The ORGANIC GARDEN PROBLEM SOLVER

JACKIE FRENCH

Angus&Robertson
An imprint of HarperCollins*Publishers*

An Angus & Robertson Publication

Angus & Robertson, an imprint of
HarperCollins *Publishers*
25 Ryde Road, Pymble, Sydney 2073, Australia
31 View Road Glenfield, Auckland 10, New Zealand

First published in Australia in 1994

National Library of Australia
Cataloguing-in Publication data:

French, Jacqueline.
  The organic garden problem solver.
  Includes index.
  ISBN 0 207 18031 8.
  1. Organic gardening. 2. Organic fertilizers.
  3. Garden pests - Biological control.
  I. Title.
635.0484

Cover design by Darian Causby
Line illustrations by Dianne Bradley

Printed in Australia

9 8 7 6 5 4 3 2 1
97 96 95 94

CONTENTS

CHAPTER ONE

ORGANIC GARDENING

I first wrote *The Organic Garden Problem Solver* with some hesitation. Good gardening isn't about control or eradication; it's about learning the natural processes of growing things. If you need to use this book often, or for longer than a couple of years while good soil and predators are established, there is something fundamentally wrong with your gardening.

As a new organic gardener, you may doubt that you'll ever get a crop at all. Even as an experienced organic gardener, you'll have times when — because of unusual weather, the introduction of a new pest in the district, or indiscriminate spraying nearby — problems will arise which need to be resolved fast. This is a book of bandaids: techniques to use while you develop other ways of coping.

Most of our gardening techniques are remnants from the days when there was plenty of garden labour (or little else to do at weekends). White Australians inherited their gardening traditions from nineteenth century Europe; a tradition of neat, dug gardens, fanatical elimination of weeds and preferably twenty gardeners to do all the work.

Nowadays herbicides and pesticides have replaced a lot of that labour but our basic growing techniques have not changed.

Fifteen years ago I learnt to garden with a wombat and a cup of tea. The wombat and I would have breakfast every morning. while the sunlight slowly slid down to the valley. I spent time just *watching* the garden and orchard: how the seedling fruit trees flourished outside my orchard without the feeding and pruning that their parents had had; how the Christmas beetles ignored the trees surrounded by wattle and hymenanthera but devastated others a few metres away; how yellow robins ate the aphids, and small wasps cleared up the pear and cherry slug and the caterpillars on the cabbages; how the potatoes next to the perennial peas did not seem to need fertilising at all.

This is wilderness gardening, a concept I have gradually developed over the past twenty years. A wilderness garden is one where the plants do the work. (See my book, *The Wilderness Garden,* Aird Books.) All a garden needs is to be planted, fed occasionally and enjoyed. You don't have to weed the garden;

instead, learn techniques of weed control and how to learn to live with weeds. You don't have to dig; digging is backbreaking. It breaks down the soil structure, leaving hard soil clumps and killing earthworms, soil bacteria, mycorrhizal and other useful soil life. Forget about watering every second day, and about artificial herbicides and pesticides. Most pest control is unnecessary, as well as dangerous, eradicating pest predators and their food supply, leaving no natural controls for pest plagues. Most of the time, with good gardening strategies, most problems will look after themselves. Gardens should be places of love and enjoyment, not places to sweat and labour.

With a little planning — and the ability to break away from gardening stereotypes — you can become a hunter–gatherer in your backyard, sitting in the sun or harvesting the garden's bounty.

SEVEN STEPS TO A HEALTHY GARDEN

1. Create a diverse garden. The more species your garden has — from birds to hoverflies, from frogs, lizards and wombats to earthworms and mycorrhizal infections around plants roots — the healthier and more able to resist drought, pests, diseases and other stresses the garden will be.

Plant a diversity of crops, especially flowering and native shrubs and trees; be more tolerant of weeds; have plenty of hiding places for lizards and frogs; provide water for birds; properly manage dogs and cats which will keep birds, frogs and lizards from the open growing areas.

2. Feed soil well. Hungry plants are prone to pests and diseases. Avoid high-nitrogen artificial fertilisers; these promote soft, sappy growth which attracts pests and diseases.

Organic growing is based on the slow, steady release of nutrients from organic matter: mulch, green manure and compost. As far as possible, let the garden grow its own fertility: nitrogen-fixing plants such as perennial sweet peas, lupins, broad beans or wattles or broom, which you can slash for mulch. Recycle everything from weeds to garbage. (Nothing is really garbage in an organic garden.)

Mulching

3. Create rich soil life. Microorganisms will either inhibit pathogens or increase plants' resistance to them. Dig as little as possible; leave organic material on the surface to rot naturally or be pulled under by earthworms and other foragers. Make sure there is always some organic matter gently rotting on the ground surface.

4. Study your garden. Watch how plants grow: when the silvereyes or the Christmas beetles arrive, how fast the soil dries in summer and when the shoots spring up in warmer weather. The best gardening is almost instinctive — a gentle touch to correct a problem before the worst symptoms appear.

5. Love your garden. The more time you spend in, and enjoying, your garden, the more care and understanding it will receive. Plants have grown and seeded and fruited for thousands of years without human assistance. It's time to watch and learn from them.

6. Concentrate on growing not killing. Avoid herbicides. These have only been used widely for about twenty-five years, so data on their impact is still being accumulated. There are many arguments about herbicides such as 245T and their possible toxic, carcinogenic, teratogenic or mutagenic effects. Any herbicide — directly dangerous to humans or not — may have harmful and lasting consequences in the environment, through unintended spreading, phototoxicity, reduced species richness, long-term changes in diversity and growing plant resistance to herbicides. Herbicides have reduced the need to rotate crops, so that continuous monoculture of the same crop is possible, which eventually leads to reduced yields as crop-specific pathogens and parasites build up in the soil. Unfortunately, the usual response is to increase fertiliser and water rather than to change the cropping system. Herbicides aren't necessary if the garden is well manured.

Avoid plant stress. Healthy plants have fewer pests and are less susceptible to disease, frost, drought and other problems. Feed and water plants properly, tend them well and they should flourish. Energy spent on pest control is better spent tending the plants. Try traps and mechanical means before anything toxic, and try the gentler pesticides and fungicides — pikelet spray or chamomile tea — before Bordeaux mixture or pyrethrum or garlic spray. Try specific remedies before more general pesticides.

Avoid pesticides wherever possible, even organic ones. The best way to encourage pests is to use pesticides; pests become resistant faster than the predators, creating an escalating problem. Once you spray — even with an organic pesticide that breaks down quickly — you may have to keep on spraying. A few pests means a few predators, ready to build up in numbers if seasonal conditions create a population explosion of pests.

7. Tolerate a little damage. Not every insect is an enemy. Some insects benefit plants directly, some clear up pests. Insects are either predators of pests or food for predators, which will in turn help to control your pest plagues. All insects are to be cherished until crop damage makes it impossible to do so; then try to control them, not eliminate them.

Wait for natural predators or good growing techniques to solve problems. There may be holes in the cabbage leaves, black spot on the roses, but your garden will probably be productive and safe, and your garden will gradually establish its own balance.

COMPANION PLANTING

A great many companion planting myths abound, such as growing marigolds to repel nematodes. Marigolds *can* repel nematodes: they'll repel them away from the marigold roots and right into the arms of the poor flowers or vegetables. Tomatoes grown with basil do not do any better or any worse than those grown without it, but if basil is condemmed to live next to tomatoes it will probably get black spot. So many companion planting hints have been passed on from book to book, all based on European observations. Australia has quite different pests and predators; garden relationships and companion planting that work overseas may not succeed here.

To know whether one plant really grows better or worse with another, grow at least two similar plots, e.g. one with tomatoes

Companion planting

without basil, one with both tomatoes and basil and perhaps a third with only basil. Take notes: measure how long the seed takes to germinate, how fast the seedlings grow, when they fruit, how much and how often. Compare each plot's performance and repeat the process next year.

Companion planting *can* very effectively reduce the need to weed, fertilise and use pesticides. This year, for example, I planted pansies with onions. Onions are slow growing and are easily overcome by weeds but the spreading, faster growing pansies kept the weeds down and insulated the soil around the onion bulbs. We got bigger and more onions for much less work. The pansies were pretty, too, and may have been protected from aphids and fungal problems by the onions. This is the essence of companion planting: designing a system where the plants do the work.

FERTILISING

Many plants 'fix' nitrogen from the air or, more correctly, the bacteria associated with their roots do. Use these plants as green manure to add fertility to the soil, to develop organic matter and to help clean up weeds, pests and diseases.

We grow masses of perennial climbing sweet peas, lovely pink and white ones which come up every year and flower through most of summer. In autumn, we feed their debris to nearby trees or vegetables. I also use the trimmings from our wattle trees as fertiliser/mulch. It is nitrogen-rich and breaks down quickly into wonderful black soil which worms adore. (A light prune keeps the wattles healthier, too.) Try growing peas, beans, lupins, broad beans and other nitrogen fixers, and using the old plants to fertilise others next door. Slash the plants as soon as they flower (before they've put most of their effort into next year's seeds), when they are rich in nutrients. Other nitrogen-fixers include casuarinas, honey locusts, sweet peas, soy beans, clover, peanuts, kennedias, broom (use sterile varieties that do not spread), woad and tree lucerne. Tree lucerne can be kept severely pruned and the prunings make excellent mulch.

WEEDING

Many plants suppress the growth of other plants, or inhibit the germination of their seeds. A plant wants to ensure that its own progeny survive and will do its best to wipe out the competition.

Every spring I let some of my radishes, as well as cabbages and other brassicas, go to seed. These flowering vegetables suppress the growth of everything around them. Then I water the garden, pull the vegetables out and have a relatively weed-free garden, already dug over by the deep roots, ready for planting. The old radishes and cabbages can rot down to become mulch later in the year.

I use a thick barrier of marigolds to suppress any couch grass that might invade the garden beds, and a thick hedge of comfrey to keep out kikuyu. The comfrey dies down each winter, about the same time the kikuyu stops growing. I slash the comfrey three or four times each summer for rich, home-grown mulch. (Don't ever dig around comfrey: it spreads.)

Be wary of some growth suppressors, however. Sunflowers suppress the growth of most plants around them, which is wonderful for clearing up a weedy patch, but not so good for other plants clustered beneath them. I sometimes grow climbing beans up our sunflowers. The plants are never as tall or as prolific as those grown elsewhere, but they produce beans up to two weeks earlier (good for an early crop) and the sunflowers seem to do better with the beans.

ATTRACTING PREDATORS

Predators, from birds to dragonflies to tiny Australian wasps, can control all pests. Many garden predators are blossom feeders and their larvae like to eat pests. Birds also adore blossom. They eat it directly and they feed on the insects that are attracted to blossom. Then they move onto nearby vegetables and clean up the insects there, too. Birds are great opportunists; even nectar feeders may eat pests when they are nesting.

Every garden needs blossom all year round. The best blossoming plants for attracting birds and other predators are probably those with tubular flowers (my favourite is pineapple sage, with its sweet-smelling leaves, brilliant red flowers and clouds of tiny birds), or any of the prolific native flowerers, as most predators are natives, too. Grevilleas provide wonderful blossom, especially those which flower most of the year, such as Robyn Gordon, but a word of warning: many people are allergic to grevilleas, especially the hybrids of *G. banksii*.

CONFUSING PESTS

Pests recognise their food supply either by its shape or by its scent. Confuse them: don't plant straight rows of anything. Mix up plants so that there are not great blocks of any one shape or scent; plant flowers among the vegetables and vegetables among the flowers for a productive, beautiful, pest-deceiving garden.

For more information on tested companion planting strategies, see my book, *Companion Planting in Australia and New Zealand* (Aird Books).

PREDATORS

Most pests need to be controlled, not eradicated. The secret is to keep the pests within reasonable bounds while the predator population builds up to match them.

A couple of years ago I grew 2,000 cauliflowers and with them came the cabbage white butterflies and their offspring, happily munching through the foliage. I squashed the caterpillars by hand and left their corpses on the leaves. After about ten days I noticed munched leaves but no caterpillars, and soon after that a steady stream of wasps and yellow robins, all busy harvesting the caterpillars. The butterflies kept laying, the caterpillars kept hatching and the predators kept eating and I was eventually able to harvest unblemished cauliflowers. This is natural pest control.

ATTRACTING PREDATORS

Water. Create a small, still pond surrounded by plants and moist soil or even an above-ground bird bath with leafy shrubs around it. Some predators, for instance dragonflies and damsel flies, breed near water; others, such as ichneumons and most birds, need to drink.

Year-round blossom. The adult forms of many predators feed on blossom, not pests, and blossom will attract other insects (not necessarily pests) that will also attract insect eaters. The best blossom is vegetable gone to seed, preferably umbelliferae. I let parsnips and dill seed most of the year in the garden. The next best blossom is provided by native shrubs, as most predators are natives too.

Low pesticide usage. Pesticides kill predators as well as pests. Without insects to feed on, predators cannot survive.

Limited digging. Many predator eggs and nymphs live in the soil, so the less you dig the more predators will survive. Regular ploughing produces dust and helps increase mite and other pest populations, because the dust kills small parasites without affecting the pests.

Controlled cats and bees. Cats kill lizards, frogs, toads, dragonflies, mantises, birds and other predators. A large number of bees may compete with hoverflies for nectar.

Honeydew. Many adult predators feed on honeydew as well as nectar. Honeydew is the sweet secretions of sap-suckers such as scale, aphids, etc., and can promote sooty mould. Tolerate a little sooty mould if possible; unless it covers more than a quarter of the plant, it should do minimal harm and is mostly a cosmetic problem.

OTHER WAYS TO ATTRACT PREDATORS:
• Provide nesting boxes. These are used in US tobacco crops for pollistes wasps as well as birds. The wasps are sheltered from bird and other predators (as well as spray drift) in the boxes.

• Spray plants with a yeast and sugar solution. This can help attract lacewings, hoverflies and other sugar-lovers to your garden. A diluted Marmite or Vegemite spray is excellent.

• Strip harvest. US lucerne trials showed that strip harvesting (harvesting only one strip at a time) conserved both pests and predators.

• Let crop residues break down naturally. Burning crop residues can kill parasitised pests before the parasites can hatch to feed on the pests of the following crop.

• Tolerate some weeds. Weeds provide habitats for natural enemies and can attract pests away from crops. Some predators can be gently transferred to plants as needed.

COMMON PREDATORS

ANTS

While ants may carry sap-sucking pests onto plants to feed on their sugary secretions, they are also useful predators which feed on many insects, particularly caterpillars, various larvae, fruit fly, codling moth and other maggots in the soil. The predatory ant *Myrmecia varians* eats large quantities of psyllids and other small insects.

The sweet sap of some acacias appears to attract ants; the ants get food and shelter from the trees and the trees are protected from insect attack and competition as the ants clear the ground around the tree. Where possible, leave ants alone in the garden. If necessary control them with grease bands.

BEETLES

Soldier beetle larvae eat codling moth and other larvae, as well as a wide range of sap suckers and locust, grasshopper and fly eggs. Soldier beetles are up to 18 mm long, with a small semi-triangular head and long body. They range in colour from yellow through to dull orange to blueish black. Soldier beetle eggs are laid on the ground.

Calosoma schayeri, or tiger beetles, feed on army and cutworms, shredding them in their tough jaws. Tiger beetles and their larvae eat a wide range of insects, mostly large ones. Some are nocturnal and will also eat codling moths.

Flower-dwelling beetles range from bright blue to bright yellow. They are mostly carnivorous.

Most of Australia's 300 described *Clerid* beetles are pest eaters, both as adults and larvae, and the larvae in particular are avid predators of wood-boring beetles. The beetles range from about 15 to 40 mm and may bite if handled. Many are brightly coloured and patterned.

Attracting beetles: Plant nectar-producing flowers and provide water.

BUGS

Assassin bugs (not assassin flies) eat beetles, grasshoppers and caterpillars. There are about 240 species so far described in Australia. Most are about 17 mm long, brown or reddish-brown to black; some are flat and some mantis-like. Some have attractive markings.

CENTIPEDES

Centipedes eat caterpillars, slugs and other pests. They have only one leg per segment. Do not confuse them with plant-eating millipedes, which have more than one leg per segment.

DAMSEL FLIES

The nymphs and adults consume large quantities of aphids and other sap-suckers. Damsel flies are very similar to dragonflies, but more delicate, slower-moving and smaller-eyed. They hold their wings erect when resting; dragonflies' wings remain horizontal. Neither damsel flies nor dragonflies sting.

DRAGONFLIES

Dragonflies are excellent mosquito predators and will catch other insects on the wing, mostly bees, mosquitoes and robber flies, but also butterflies. I have seen them catch cabbage white butterflies and even Christmas beetles. They are perhaps the world's fastest insects; they can fly at 14 metres per second.

Attracting damsel flies and dragonflies: As the eggs of both are laid either in water or, in some species, poked into plants growing near water, they may be attracted to a pond or dam surrounded by plants.

EARWIGS

Earwigs mostly feed on detritus. One species feeds on codling moth larvae. Damage to seedlings is usually minimal; damage to buds may be greater. Earwigs can also be a nuisance indoors. See Roses, p. 122 for control if necessary.

FROGS AND TOADS

Frogs and toads are becoming endangered in Australia. They eat insects, slugs and snails.
Attracting frogs and toads: Provide moist, leafy, shady spots. Control cats, which kill frogs and toads.

LONG-HORNED GRASSHOPPERS

These are known as katydids in the US. Some species eat other insests, though most are herbivorous. There are about 300 species in Australia.

HOVERFLIES

Hoverflies are perhaps the best predators of all for aphids. They also eat a wide range of scale insects, mites and possibly small larvae such as pear and cherry slug and young caterpillars. The many different hoverflies vary substantially in appearance: some are like small thick bees, others like thin-waisted wasps. They can be recognised by their distinctive hovering and are mostly seen in spring and summer.

Hoverfly larvae can eat 1 aphid in a minute, 50 a day and up to 900 in their lifetime. They actively seek out their prey, range widely and are active at lower temperatures than other aphid predators such as ladybirds and their larvae.
Attracting hoverflies: Plant flowering plants, especially in late winter and spring. Try flowering brassicas: let cabbages or broccoli go to seed, but cut off the tops just before the seeds set, so new flower heads form. Buckwheat flowers attract hoverflies, as do melon and zucchini flowers, flowering sages, flowering dill and parsnips (let these go to seed and they will self-sow perpetually) and almost any spring-flowering annual.

A warning to beekeepers: in late winter/ early spring I have noticed bees repulsing hoverflies which compete for the same flowers.

ICHNEUMONS

These parasites, often called either flies or wasps, lay eggs in many pests. They eat caterpillars, including cabbage moth and cabbage white caterpillars, and codling moth larvae; they will also eat sawfly larvae and pear and cherry slug. They have long wasp-like legs, narrow waists and are often banded. They are orange to yellow and are mostly around 30–40 mm long. A common species is *Netelia productus*.

LACEWINGS

Both the adults and their larvae eat a wide range of garden pests, including aphids, scale, mealy bugs, mites, whitefly, thrips, pear and cherry slug and on occasion codling moth larvae. Green lacewing larvae feed only on aphids; another lacewing preys mostly on spotted or red spider mites. Lacewings also feed on a range of other sap-sucking insects, on butterfly and moth eggs and the egg capsules of spiders.

There are about 400 species of lacewings recorded in Australia. They can be distinguished by their transparent, slightly metallic wings. Some lacewings lay their eggs on a fine thread or stalk, two or three times as long as the egg. The eggs hatch in about two weeks and the carnivorous larvae live in garden debris on the ground. Antlions are the larvae of the antlion lacewing. They make deep pits to trap insects.
Attracting lacewings: Mix Vegemite and water into a weak tea-coloured spray and douse plants in it. Vegetables going to seed, especially parsnips and radishes, attract lacewings. A garden that is well mulched and not regularly disturbed will help more lacewing larvae survive to maturity.

LADYBIRDS

Both ladybird larvae and many adult ladybirds are pest predators. On hatching, ladybird larvae begin to eat scale, aphids, whitefly, mealy bugs, woolly aphids and other sap-suckers. One ladybird larva may eat a hundred aphids and several thousand aphid larvae. Ladybirds have been introduced in various areas for biological control.

Ladybirds vary in colour from orange and red to blue or green. More than 250 species have been described in Australia so far. Some are leaf eaters, most notably the 28-spotted ladybird, which may eat tomato, potato and pepito foliage. Treasure all other ladybirds.

Attracting ladybirds: Avoid using oil, Bordeaux, derris and pyrethrum sprays, which can wipe out ladybirds; try rhubarb spray instead. If using oil or Bordeaux sprays, spray every second tree, wait ten days, then spray the rest. This way a residual ladybird population survives to build up for spring.

LIZARDS

These eat slugs, snails, flies and other insects, depending on the type of lizard.

Attracting lizards: Provide them with rocky places and a good thick bush garden. Protect them from cats.

PARASITES

A wide range of parasites exists for all insect pests. While parasites usually do not kill pests, they make them vulnerable to predators. Little can be done to increase parasitism, with a few exceptions mentioned in the text.

PRAYING MANTISES

Young mantises eat aphids and leafhoppers; old mantises eat caterpillars, bugs, beetles and sometimes moths and other insects. Australia has over 100 species of praying mantis. The most common are green and brown and can be distinguished from locusts by their 'praying' position, with their strong forelegs lifted up. Mantises are active during both night and day, and their green and brown colour camouflages them well.

Attracting mantises: Do not disturb mantis eggs, which are laid in a frothy mass attached to a surface like a tree or fence. To protect the eggs from being parasitised by wasps, keep them in an open jar indoors. They will hatch in four to six months; on hatching, separate the mantises immediately or they will eat each other. Although mantises are carnivorous they can be raised on raw apple, potato and other raw fruit, live or dead insects and crumbs of meat. Use a netted fish tank, with only one mantis at a time in each (they can turn cannibal). Once established, adult mantises tend to stay put if they have enough food and as long as there is no mantis-catching cat nearby.

ROBBER AND ASSASSIN FLIES

These flies eat any insect they can catch, mostly flying insects. They will also sting humans. They are long, thin, hairy flies, with thick legs and wingspans ranging from 2 to 75 mm. The larvae are cyclindrical grubs living in soil or old timber.

SCORPION FLIES

These prey on flies, bees, caterpillars and beetle larvae. They pupate just below the soil. Only the males are predatory, securing insects to feed the females during mating. The females otherwise feed on nectar.

The many scorpion flies in Australia vary considerably in appearance, from lacewing-like to cockroach-like. They all have long spindly legs and long transparent wings with opaque veins, with the wings held over the abdomen like a tent when they are resting.

Attracting scorpion flies: Plant nectar-producing plants; provide damp or marshy places, preferably with water and undisturbed soil, for pupating.

SPIDERS

Spiders live almost entirely on insects, not just web-caught flies and mosquitoes. They will eat caterpillars, including codling moth larvae, flying termites, butterflies, whiteflies and many others.

STILT FLIES

These will feed on aphids. They are small, thin, tapering flies with wingspans of up to 15 mm, green to brown in colour with long, thin legs. *Attracting stilt flies:* Provide damp and wet places, and plenty of foliage.

TACHINID FLIES

These pollinate plants as well as preying on a wide range of pests. Their larvae are parasitic in the bodies of beetles and moths. The adults resemble thick-bodied, bristly blowflies, some much smaller and some much larger than house flies. Do not kill any flies until you are sure that they are houseflies or common blowflies.

WASPS

Many species of wasps either prey on or parasitise pests (or their eggs). They eat a wide range of caterpillars, including those of the cabbage white butterfly, pear and cherry slug and codling moth. Some wasps also attack scale. Chalcid wasps (metallic blue, black or brown and about 1 mm long), parasitise beetles and mealy bugs as well as a range of eggs, scale and caterpillars.

I have watched ground wasps carry away enormous quantities of cabbage white butterflies as well as pear and cherry slugs. Ground wasps dig burrows in the sand. The large orange and black wasp grows up to 35 mm long. Having accidentally sat on one I can say that while not at all aggressive they do sting, but not too severely.

Flower wasps are are excellent predators of scarab beetles and their larvae and many other moth larvae. They are mostly large, hairy and bright blue and are attracted by a wide range of flowers.

Paper wasps eat caterpillars, spiders, pear and cherry slugs and aphids. Some paper wasps are common wasps, with thin combed nests hung from a slender stalk. Others are rarer. All build their nests out of chewed wood 'paper'. Some will give a painful sting but they are not aggressive.

Mud wasps prey on caterpillars, spiders and possibly other pests. They grow up to 30 mm long and have conspicuously slender waists. One of the most common mud wasps is orange with a black band (not to be confused with the European wasp). They build clay nests, often on the walls of buildings.

Club or cicada hunter sphecid wasps eat a wide range of pests. The 420 species so far described in Australia eat caterpillars, locusts, beetles, spiders and other insects, depending on the size of the wasps and the prey.

Note: not all wasps sting, so don't automatically spray them.

BIRDS AS PEST CONTROLLERS

Birds are the most adaptable pest predators of all. Unlike most insect predators they move from one food supply to another depending on its abundance. Birds will often eat up to 40% of a pest on a plant. Here, I have watched yellow robins completely clearing aphids off a rose, kookaburras gulping snails all morning, blue wrens guzzling caterpillars, bee eaters snapping cabbage white butterflies, and grey currawongs knocking back adult Christmas beetles. There can, however, be a time lag. Don't expect pest problems to be solved as soon birds arrive.

ATTRACTING BIRDS

WATER

Nearly all birds need water (some survive on flower nectar), and free-standing water is usually in short supply in suburban gardens. Some birds, like willy wagtails, like to nest

near water. Water also attracts many insects —
more food for birds.

Water should be deep enough so that birds
can bathe. Make sure there is a place for birds
to perch and drink. Even small containers of
water will supply many birds; they have
pecking orders and will drink one after
another. Water should be fresh; try a dripper
attached to some half-inch black plastic pipe,
continually refreshing the bird bath or pond.

All water should be out of the reach of
cats. One way of making a simple cat-proof
bird drinker is to suspend a container of water
on a rope, e.g. an ice cream container with
the lid glued to the bottom as a perch. Bigger
bird baths should have sloping sides or a rock
in the middle so birds can bathe there as well
as drink. Leptospermums or other shrubs may
be placed near bird baths as they provide good
landing places. Do not do this if there are cats
nearby.

Ponds should have a boulder or other
drinking place a few metres in from the edge,
where cats cannot leap to them. Let ponds slope
gently, with boggy reedy areas at the edges,
again to attract insects as well as water birds.

Broken light is best for bird baths; the water
is kept relatively cool and the semi-shade may
give small birds a feeling of security.

SHELTER

Small birds need shelter from larger birds, cats,
dogs, etc. Plant shrubs close together to form
thickets. Try prickly plants like grevilleas and
hakeas. Use native grasses and grass-like plants
to encourage nesting. Make sure you have
'landing' trees, too (dead or leafless or open-
branched trees); eucalypts are excellent.

CATS

I love cats, but every cat catches birds, lizards,
frogs and other predators. They are simply not
compatible with natural Australian gardens. To
control neighbouring cats, either fence them

out with overhanging wire or spray them with
the hose when they appear in your garden.

If you have an indispensable cat:
• Feed your cat small regular meals and always
have dry food available so it never hunts from
hunger.

• Discourage it from catching birds with
whatever punishment you usually give it
(disapproval may be enough). Try also covering
dead decoy birds with chilli paste.

•Train it to seek amusement from toys,
dangling wool, etc. Most cats hunt for
interest, not food.

See also Cats, pp. 44–45.

While dogs may chase birds, they cannot
climb, and a dog may keep your garden cat-
free. Many birds are also fond of dog food.

PERCHES

Birds like to perch. Some, such as owls and
kookaburras, need high lookouts like pergolas
or gum tree branches. Some like low, prickly,
protected bushes. Provide a variety of perches.

NESTS

Birds may nest in tree hollows, mud banks,
grass, reeds, prickly shrubs, etc. Tree hollows
and prickly shrubs are the two most
common nesting places. If you don't have
tree hollows, make one: hollow out a piece
of wood and tie it to a branch. Hollow
crevices can be made the same way. Birds
usually dislike bird houses, although some
do like eaves.

PESTICIDES

Many pesticides are cumulative: they are passed
on up the food chain. Birds may be affected by
pesticide-killed insects or by infected water.
They may die or be rendered infertile, or
simply be driven elsewhere by lack of food.

FOOD

Food for birds needs to be permanently available. Make sure you have flowers, seeds, fruit or whatever the bird population needs the year round. This is best achieved by providing a constant succession of flowering shrubs which will fruit and seed in their turns.

Nectar-producing plants not only feed nectar-eating birds, but attract insects for the insect-eating birds. Many nectar-eating birds eat insects during nesting, or when there is a plague of insects. In addition, many adult predators such as wasps and hoverflies feed on nectar. Flowering plants will attract them and other predators such as tachinid flies.

One reliable way to attract birds is to provide supplementary food on a bird table. Don't worry that birds may starve if you stop feeding them. According to studies at the University of Maryland, even regularly fed birds regard their 'human meals' as luxuries, not as their staple diet, and better fed birds are often better able to forage.

PESTS AND THEIR PREDATORS

APHIDS
Birds: Cuckoo shrikes, eastern spinebills (sometimes), firetails, grey shrike thrushes, honeyeaters, house sparrows, kingfishers (sometimes), pardalotes, silvereyes, some finches during nesting, thornbills, tree creepers, whistlers, willy wagtails (like to nest near water), wrens (prefer low branches or tussocks to nest in), yellow and other robins.
Other: Damsel bugs, hoverflies, lacewings (especially green lacewings); ladybird larvae, paper wasps, stilt flies.

BEANFLIES
Birds: See Aphids above.
Other: Ants, damsel bugs, hoverflies, lacewings, ladybirds and their larvae, mantises, stilt flies, wasps.

BEETLES
Birds: Black cockatoos, currawongs, owls, tree creepers.
Other: Assassin bugs, dragonflies, mantises, scorpion flies, tachinid flies, wasps.

BORERS
Birds: Black cockatoos (these strip bark off to eat the pests), currawongs, sitellas, tree creepers.
Other: Assassin bugs, Clerid beetles, dragonflies, scorpion flies (eat larvae), wasps, tachinid flies.

BUGS
Birds: Black cockatoos, currawongs and kookaburras eat juvenile bugs only.
Other: Assassin flies, dragonflies, mantises, robber flies.

CATERPILLARS
Birds: Cicada birds, cuckoos, flycatchers, grey shrike thrushes, magpies, choughs, magpie larks, currawongs, monarchs, noisy miners, pardalotes, Richard's pippits, rosellas, rufous whistlers; starlings (sometimes), trillers, yellow robins.
Other: Ants, assassin bugs, centipedes, dragonflies (also eat butterflies and moths), ichneumons, scorpion flies, spiders, tachinid flies, wasps.

CHRISTMAS BEETLES
Birds: Grey currawongs, magpies.
Other: Assassin bugs, dragonflies, mantises, scorpion flies, tachinid flies, wasps.

Control slug and snail damage to cabbages by using barriers,
snail fences, traps, baits and repellents. Birds will also help reduce pest numbers.

Flowering parsnip and garlic plants attract useful predators
such as hoverflies and small native wasps.

Gardens with a good population of worms and insects will attract pest-controlling birds such as blue wrens.

CODLING MOTHS
Birds: Nightjars, owls, swifts.
Other: Ants, beetles, earwigs (eat the larvae), ichneumons, lacewings and their larvae, spiders, tachinid flies, wasps. Many caterpillar eaters eat the larvae stage of codling moth.

CUTWORMS
Birds: Currawongs, kookaburras, magpies.
Other: Ants, Calosoma beetles and tiger beetles, spiders, soil-dwelling larvae.

FRUIT FLIES
Birds: Willy wagtails (but with limited effect.)
Other: Ants and predatory flies may catch them on the wing; otherwise, introduced fruit flies have few natural predators.

GRASSHOPPERS AND LOCUSTS
Birds: Bustards, cuckoos, fantails, free range hens which are used to hunting their food, honeyeaters, kingfishers, noisy friar birds, owls, Richard's pippits, scarlet and yellow robins, straw-necked ibises, willy wagtails.
Other: Assassin bugs, soldier beetles, sphecid wasps.

HELIOTHIS CATERPILLARS
Birds: Cicada birds, cuckoos, flycatchers, grey shrike thrushes, magpies, choughs, magpie larks, currawongs, monarchs, noisy miners, pardalotes, Richard's pippits, rosellas, rufous whistlers; starlings (sometimes), trillers, yellow robins.
Other: Assassin bugs, caterpillars, centipedes, dragonflies, hoverflies (eat small caterpillars), ichneumons, lacewings (which eat the eggs), mantises, scorpion flies, spiders, wasps.

LERPS
Birds: Blue wrens, cuckoo shrikes, some finches during nesting, firetails, honeyeaters.
Other: Predator ants, lacewing larvae, wasps.

MITES
Birds: See Aphids, p. 12.

Other: Ants, damsel bugs, hoverflies, lacewings, ladybirds and their larvae, mantises, stilt flies, wasps.

PEAR AND CHERRY SLUGS
Birds: Cuckoo shrikes, currawongs, firetails, magpies (eat larvae); scarlet and yellow robins, silvereyes, thornbills (sometimes).
Other: Christmas beetles, lacewings, ichneumons, wasps.

SAWFLIES
Birds: Cuckoos, currawongs, magpies, noisy miners, robins, shrike thrushes, wrens.
Other: Hoverflies, ichneumons, lacewings (eat the eggs), spiders, wasps.

SCALE
Birds: Blue wrens, cuckoo shrikes, firetails, honeyeaters, pardalotes, silvereyes, some finches during nesting, tree creepers.
Other: Chalcid wasps, damsel bugs, hoverflies, lacewings, ladybird larvae.

SNAILS
Birds: Butcher birds, chooks, currawongs, ducks, glossy ibises, kookaburras, magpies (sometimes), mynahs (sometimes), nightjars, owls (sometimes), pittas, trillers (sometimes).
Other: Beetles (eat snail eggs), centipedes, frogs, lizards, toads.

THRIPS
Birds: Blue wrens, cuckoo shrikes, firetails, honeyeaters, pardalotes, Richard's pippits, shrike thrushes, thornbills, tree creepers, whistlers, wood swallows (as they dip for nectar).
Other: Damsel bugs, lacewings and their larvae, ladybird larvae, spiders.

WHITEFLIES
Birds: Cuckoo shrikes, house sparrows, finches during nesting, willy wagtails (like to nest near water), yellow and other robins.
Other: Spiders.

CHAPTER TWO

ENVIRONMENTAL PROBLEMS

FERTILITY

The healthier the soil, the fewer insect pests and diseases your plants will have. (Unfortunately you will still get possum, rabbit and bird damage.)

About fifteen years ago I planted sixty-seven peach trees. They were in wet soil at the bottom of the orchard. They got curly leaf, aphids, red spider mites, root rots; every pest or disease around. The others, right next door but on good soil, well-fed and mulched, were untouched.

If you doubt, try it yourself. Grow two beds, side by side, identical except for the feeding. Make one bed out of compost, feed the other with artificial fertiliser. Count the pests, note the diseases. You'll probably be able to taste the difference in the crops, too.

A few years ago some friends began a new garden. The first year it was devastated with every pest around, but they kept on adding compost and refused to spray. The second year there was a lot of pest damage, but some crops survived. The third year there were still pests, but not in harmful numbers.

TO FEED SOIL:

1. Recycle. Turn garbage into compost, throw weeds and prunings under big trees or scatter them among other crops as mulch, and leave lawn clippings to feed your lawn.

2. Grow nitrogen-fixing plants with your crops. See Fertilising, p. 4.

3. Scavenge useful mulch. Other people's leaves, lawn clippings and even scraps from grocers or restaurants can be used for compost or hen food (see Compost, p. 15.)

4. Buy mulch. It will feed the soil, help control disease and perhaps increase frost resistance. Bales of lucerne hay are as cheap as artificial fertiliser, but you get a lot more for your money.

5. Buy blood and bone, pelletised manures and other organic fertilisers. These should be used as treats rather than as part of a regular diet.

6. Keep hens. It's cheaper to buy food for hens than to buy hen manure, and naturally deposited manure is better for your soil. Hens provide eggs and entertainment in addition to their manure and will clean up kitchen scraps with dedication. Rabbits and guinea pigs kept in cages are also useful in the organic garden.

7. Use liquid fertiliser. Vegetables such as lettuce, silverbeet or celery need frequent fertilising. Make a liquid fertiliser by soaking compost, comfrey, seaweed, nettles, manure or lucerne hay in water. (Store in a bucket with the lid on as it may smell or breed mosquitoes otherwise.) Dispose of the mixture if it starts to bubble and ferment. When it is a weak tea colour, use the liquid every few days on plants. If it is much darker than tea colour, dilute it with more water first. It is also possible to add some *fresh* urine (no older than 2–3 hours) to this brew just before watering. Make sure the urine is diluted with nine parts of water and that it is fresh, or the plants will be burnt. Don't use urine which may be infected or very salty (i.e. if the urine donor has a high-salt diet). Don't use urine on any one spot more than three times per season, or the soil may get too salty, as all urine contains some salt.

COMPOST

Compost is better than anything else for making plants grow. But there is a daunting mystique about making compost, with myths about turning it every third day, and using esoteric herbs or expensive starter kits. There is also the turn-off of seeing so-called compost piles (in reality just piles of rubbish) breeding flies down the back yard. Compost breaks down fast. If it does not, it is not compost, just a pile of weeds and scraps.

Why make compost? It's cheap and probably the best fertiliser and soil conditioner known. Compost gives a better result than the same materials used in mulch, with nutrients that might otherwise have been lost, adding

nitrogen from nitrogen-fixing bacteria. Compost encourages earthworms, can neutralise excess acidity or alkalinity, may provide spores, living bacteria and fungi that suppress pathogens like phytophthora root rots, eelworm and potato scurf, or supply fungal spores for mycorrhizal associations that help plants grow by increasing their resistance.

Many plant nutrients such as phosphorous and potassium, locked up in the soil, are released by the organic acids produced by the microorganisms in compost. A good hot compost heap will also help control disease in garden wastes and kill off weed seeds.

COMMERCIAL GEDYE BINS
These are useful for waste storage but don't produce very good compost. Try to alternate dense moist material with light debris such as corn stalks, to increase aeration.

PLASTIC BAG COMPOST
Stuff the waste into garbage bags and seal them well. The compost is ready when the material is soft and homogenous. (The smell when the bags are opened soon vanishes.) Plastic bag compost is a good way of utilising fruit infected with codling moth or fruit fly as the bugs cannot escape the plastic bags.

LIQUID COMPOST
Fill a bucket with any of the following: green weeds, lawn clippings, green leaves, green vegetable scraps (lettuce or cabbage leaves, carrot tops, etc.), garden scraps. Comfrey leaves, seaweed or nettles help make plants healthier too. Also add fresh or stale manures if available, or a spadeful of compost.

Fill the bucket with water, and wait a week or two until it starts to turn brown. Dilute it to the colour of weak tea and pour it onto plants once a week. Add more water to the bucket and let it brew again. After a month or two the decomposed sediment at the bottom of the bucket can be used as mulch.

Liquid compost

TWO–WEEK COMPOST

Shred together vegetable matter and garden waste with a shredder, mower, garden shears, etc. Pile it about a metre high and wide. Moisten the pile with liquid manure. This is made by suspending green garden waste or seaweed or manure in a bucket and leaving for a few weeks. Take out liquid as needed and dilute to weak tea colour.

Turn the compost every two days, adding more liquid manure if it needs moistening. If it is not heating after two days it needs more nitrogen; add stronger liquid manure. The secret of this method is the frequent turning, the finely chopped ingredients and the high nitrogen level.

What material is suitable for compost? Almost anything that has once lived is suitable. In the last year our bin has been fed a dead fox, an old hat, scraps, weeds, an old doormat, newspapers, ragged jeans, many bones and some rotten hessian.

What are compost activators? Some people swear by compost activators: materials either herbal or shop-bought that are supposed to speed up compost. Well-made compost should break down so fast that activators are unnecessary. A sprig of yarrow, or some of the soil underneath yarrow, a handful of chamomile flowers or layers of comfrey leaves may help. Compost made under the drip line of an elder tree is said to do particularly well.

Should anything special be added to compost? Wood ash, egg shells or rock phosphate can be added if the soil is phosphorous-deficient. Phosphorous materials break down more slowly.

Compost tends to be slightly acidic. The problem with acid soil is not acidity, but the fact that in acid or alkaline soil some plant nutrients are not available. This may not prove a problem in compost-enriched soil. Do not add lime or dolomite, as they speed up nitrogen loss. If lime is really necessary, add it after the compost is finished.

How do I know if the compost heap is working? Compost should start to heat up after three days. If it does not, check that it is not too wet, too clagged together with old porridge or rotten oranges, too dry, or in need of air or nitrogen (if so, add some, as below). Compost should stay warm, not hot, until it is

Two-week compost

Shred materials

Moisten with liquid manure

Turn every two days

a solid mass. If it smokes or turns grey inside it is too hot; toss it around to cool it down.

When is the compost ready? When it is no longer possible to tell what went in it, except for the odd tough object.

Why has my compost failed? It might be too wet or too dry. It might not have enough air. Probably it lacked sufficient nitrogen. Most compost material is scraps or weeds or woody residues and consequently low in nitrogen. If compost fails to heat up, add nitrogen in the form of urine, dilute hen manure, blood and bone, or green leafy lucerne. Wait a few days and if it fails to heat up, add more. A bit of phosphorous helps compost speed up, too; try a sprinkle of ground rock phosphate. Toss the compost around to aerate it.

Why is my compost a pale, sludgy mess? It contains too many food scraps and not enough green matter. Add more leaves, grass clippings, corn stalks, etc.; the compost will be drier and more aerated and should start to break down.

Why does my compost stink? It has become anaerobic instead of aerobic; it needs air. Toss it around. Add more nitrogen if necessary.

Why are there fruit fly, cockroaches or mice in the compost? The compost is not sufficiently hot. It should start to heat up in three days, at most a week in cold weather. Add more nitrogenous matter and toss it around. If there are too many food or fruit scraps, add drier material.

WATER

All gardeners should conserve water, firstly because there are very few truly wet areas in Australia (most city water is transported at great financial and ecological expense). Secondly, all water has dissolved salts; watering deposits these salts in the soil where they accumulate gradually. City water in particular is often treated with chlorine and fluoride, neither of which is good for plants.

Many of our growing techniques are inherited from water-rich Europe. There are many ways to grow a lush, productive garden, even a vegetable garden, while using very little water at all.

WHY PLANTS NEED WATER

Plants consist of about 80% water, absorbing it mostly through their roots and losing it by transpiration through their leaves. Plants wilt when they can no longer take up enough water to make up their losses, either because of heat or lack of soil moisture. Eventually they can die, either from immediate stress or because without sufficient water they are unable to take up sufficient nutrients. In this last case, even if plants do survive the lack of water, they will be stunted.

Sometimes mild water stress can be good for the garden. Plants are encouraged to send down deeper roots and so become more drought-tolerant; soft, disease-prone growth is reduced and plants can be gradually 'hardened off' to the lack of water. For many fruit trees, mild water stress when flower buds are forming will increase the number of buds, although this should not continue once the buds start to develop. Less water while fruit is growing usually means smaller fruit, but the fruit may also have a better flavour, improved keeping qualities and excellent texture. Too much water when fruit is ripening can split it.

Wherever water is scarce, or expensive, the gardener's aim should be to use as little as possible without causing water stress.

HOW TO CONSERVE WATER

Water only when needed. Stick your finger in the soil or under the mulch to see if it is damp. If it is, don't water. Surface dryness is no indication of dry soil, just as a moist surface doesn't mean there is moisture below.

Water only as deep as the roots. Not all areas of the garden will need the same amount of water. Shallow-rooted plants such as strawberries and lettuce will need more frequent but shorter watering than carrots or shrubs. If in doubt dig a trench near the vegetables to about the same depth as their roots. Stop watering when the moisture has penetrated to the bottom of the trench. Alternatively, use a tensiometer, which reads the amount of moisture in the soil, and plan your watering accordingly.

Plan your watering. Water before a hot spell, if you can predict it, and not during the searing heat of the day, when most will evaporate. Don't water on windy days. To avoid powdery mildew on damp foliage, water in the evening or in the early morning.

Contrary to much gardening advice, one good watering a week may not be best for the garden. Plants prefer a constant water supply, not a weekly waterlogging. Give as much water as is needed to penetrate to the roots and water again just before the plants start to wilt.

Use drip irrigation. In hot areas more water evaporates from sprinklers than gets to the soil; the water that is absorbed will be high in dissolved salts. Drippers will use perhaps a tenth of the water with better results.

Conserve moisture through mulching. Mulch will raise the humus level of soil. This will increase both the moisture-carrying capacity of the soil and the availability of the moisture to the plants.

Mulch will also reduce evaporation and stop that thin crust forming on the soil top which can prevent moisture penetrating. Even good, humus-rich soil can repel water if it is baked hard. At the end of the drought here we had ten inches of rain in an hour, but the water simply flowed off. After the rain had stopped, the soil in most places was still dry a few centimetres down. Only where we had mulched could the water penetrate.

Any mulch, even stones and newspaper, is better than nothing. Be liberal with it.

Increase the area of shade. This will cool the garden generally (the more greenery, the less heat and light will be reflected). In hot areas broken light will keep the plants and soil below moist, and most flowers and vegetables

Mulching

will tolerate broken light. Shade can be from a pergola, from a tall trellis facing the strong afternoon light, from a tree above or from tall plants such as corn, Jerusalem artichokes or sunflowers liberally planted through the flower and vegetable beds.

Keep plants healthy. Strongly growing plants are better able to take up moisture and to cope with a temporary lack.

GREY WATER

One solution commonly suggested for water shortage in the garden is to utilise grey water. This is waste water from the house, excluding that used in the toilet. Its major advantage is that it *is* water when other water is scarce. Grey water has a lot of disadvantages. Even if grey water doesn't include water from the toilet, it may include small amounts of faecal matter and bodily wastes which have been flushed down showers, laundry tubs, etc. While most disease organisms are quickly broken down in the soil, some might be splashed onto vegetables. For this reason, grey water is probably only safe for use on trees and ornamentals.

Many kitchen wastes swept down the kitchen sink are damaging in the garden, e.g. grease and oil, which prevent moisture penetrating. Salt is also a dangerous by-product of soap and detergent, although soap and particularly soap flakes have far less sodium salt than detergents. If you plan to use grey water, avoid detergents, highly perfumed soap and water softeners and products containing boron or chlorine. Install a filter, and regularly clean out soap sludge.

Use grey water carefully (never more than a weekly bucket per square metre) and practise other moisture-conserving techniques.

DROUGHT-TOLERANT PLANTS

Plant drought-tolerant species whenever possible. Native plants are not necessarily drought-tolerant, as many originally come from high rainfall areas and need just as much water as exotics. They may only grow deep, drought-resistant roots in sandy or light soils and need constant watering on clay or shallow soils.

Features of drought-tolerant species:

• Root systems are deep and fleshy.

• Leaves are tough and thin or have a waxy or hairy coating, to reduce evaporation.

• Leaves are small and point up and down, to reduce the surface area exposed to sunlight.

• Plants shed leaves when water-stressed and grow new ones after.

• Plants open their stomata (pores in the leaves through which water can pass) only at night, e.g. cactuses and pineapples.

TRENCH GARDENS

Dig a trench no more than one metre wide or you will be unable to reach across it. Angle it east-west, so it catches the sunlight. Let the

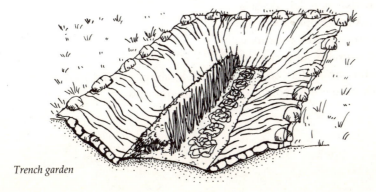

Trench garden

trench slope slightly to allow moisture to run down it. (Check whether the trench slopes by trickling water down it.) Slope the sides to catch moisture. Leave these bare or, better still, line them with plastic. Weigh the plastic down with rocks, cover with more plastic and secure with more rocks at the edges. At night the moisture in the air between the layers will condense and seep down into the garden. Now either line the trench base with a couple of centimetres of compost, or slightly disturb its surface. Plant vegetables and mulch well.

Do not use the sprinkler, because up to 90% of the water will be lost by evaporation on a hot day. Just insert the end of the hose under the mulch at the uphill end of the trench or at several points along it if it's too long.

TOO MUCH WATER

In my twenty years in this garden it has always been either a drought or too wet. We have had perhaps two years of 'proper' weather; delicious rain showers at night every few days, no floods or long brown stretches of barrenness. When it's wet here, it's very wet. The leeches advance like a barbarian horde, the fruit rots on the trees, the wombats wander round with damp coats and sniffles.

Here are some ways to cope with wet weather in the garden:

Add potash and other foods. This is the classic orchardist's trick. Potash helps new growth 'harden off' so that it is less disease prone and more frost resistant. Apply about an ounce to the square metre, or add a sprinkle of wood ash instead. Comfrey is also rich in potash; use it as mulch or add it to the compost. Fertilise with mulch and compost

that will steadily decompose when and where the plants need it. Do not dig either of these in when the soil is wet, though; any digging in wet ground destroys soil structure and undecomposed organic matter encourages root rots. Leave it on top for the worms and bacteria to return to the soil instead.

Cut the grass. Long grass encourages mildews, fungi, etc., increasing humidity at plant level. Short grass means more breeze at ground level, less moisture and less disease.

Avoid transferring infections. Many disease spores are transferred by wind, but others travel on skirts, trousers or hands. Do not brush past infected plants then wander down to the next lot. Practise garden quarantine.

Do not apply nitrogenous fertiliser. This will only result in more soft, wet growth.

Apply seaweed or green manure sprays. These will strengthen resistance to fungal infections, make plants more frost hardy and should improve fruit set.

IN VERY WET AREAS:
• Build drains on slopes above gardens to channel off moisture (these may have to be as much as a metre deep).

• Plant deep-rooted moisture-draining trees such as casuarinas and willows above ground level (slash the branches for mulch). To plant above ground, slice off the grass, build up a small heap of soil and arrange the tree roots over it; then build up soil over the roots so there is a nice gradual slope on either side.

• Build above ground gardens, so that plants' feet are out of water.

FROST

Frost itself usually does not kill plants; it is the thawing afterwards, as the swollen cells burst. There are two options with frost: protect the garden from it, or ensure gentle thawing.

The worst frost damage occurs when plants thaw rapidly. If possible, give plants a thorough gentle watering before the sun hits them. This way the plant cells gradually relax instead of bursting. Even totally frozen plants can be restored this way. Increase the thawing time by covering plants with blankets or old newspapers, either the night before or as soon as frost is visible on the ground.

As a last resort, rely on frost-hardy plants and ones that have been hardened to your area. Any plant bought from a hotter area or from an indoor area in a nursery may well tolerate less frost than a local plant. You can gradually harden plants by leaving them outside for longer periods each day. Better still, raise hardened plants from cuttings or seed saved from plants growing nearby.

HOW TO AVOID FROST

Choose frost-free sites. Judge the frost potential of the garden. Even in a small area frost damage can vary enormously. Imagine frost as a body of cold air flowing like water. It settles in hollows, flows down drains and air channels, and is easily blocked by fences, hedges and other plants. If frost can drain away it may leave higher spots in the garden clear, especially if they face north and are warmer.

My garden is on a slight slope with a ridge behind. There are enough differences in microclimate to grow raspberries and sugar maples in one part where the sun is blocked until late morning and the frost stays until midday, and to grow avocados metres away where the frost drains down a sunnier slope.

Before major plantings, watch how the frost settles in the garden. Work out whether the intended garden design will change the frost pattern; a new fence, for example, might block the frost and burn off plants previously untouched, while clearing a hedge could let frost drain away, or the slow growth of a large tree may gradually protect the plants beneath it.

Increase the frost-free area. Clear away any blockages — weed piles, solid fences or long grass or bracken round the fences — so that frost can drain away. Try cutting drainage holes low in hedges or other shrubbery.

Spray seaweed or nettle tea. A weekly spray increases plants' resistance to frost and helps fruit set in cold areas. Cover seaweed or nettles with water, leave for a few weeks and dilute to weak tea colour before spraying.

A garden designed to minimise the effects of frost

Use overhead irrigation. This releases the latent heat of the water during spraying. For this to be effective, start spraying when the temperature is still at least 2°C or more. Large-scale commercial equipment is not necessary: a garden spray or even microjets can also work well.

Use wind machines. These mix cold air with the warmer air above it. Wind machines are available commercially or can be home-made. A 10 horse-power motor driving a propellor on a 10 metre tower is claimed to raise the temperature over a hectare by 2°C in a few minutes.

Predict frost. Some gardeners swear they can smell a frost; cold, dry air has a clear, sharp smell. Frost is less likely when the sky is cloudy, and when there is fog or other moisture around. If the stars are particularly bright and twinkling there will probably be a frost following; take precautions accordingly. It is helpful to keep frost records from year to year. The dates of the first and last frost each year will be fairly consistent.

Light fires. Lighting fires around the garden is an old-fashioned way to keep off frost. With today's awareness of global warming and increased CO_2, firelighting should probably be generally avoided and is certainly not a remedy suitable for suburban areas.

HIGH–MULCHED GARDENS
Low, solid mulch attracts frost but lightly packed mulch can protect plants. Surround the garden with wire mesh or tomato stakes with string around them. Fill this circle with dry leaves or lightly packed hay so only the tops of the plants show through. The mesh should stop the leaves blowing away. Harvest crops through the mulch. Plants can dry out under this mulch and may eventually rot, so cover the garden for only the most dangerously frosty times (about six weeks in late autumn, or in early spring for late harvesting or hardening off early plants).

WATER IN GARDENS
A pond in the middle of the garden will keep the area around it slightly warmer through the night as steam rises from it. Keep your swimming pool full in winter and use it as heat storage for surrounding frost-sensitive plants.

SHELTERED GARDENS
Orange groves in England used to be planted in specially designed groves of other trees, tall and thick, that kept them sheltered. Use larger trees to protect smaller shrubs below.

TYRE GARDENING
Tyres, being thick and black, absorb and retain heat well. Get some old tyres from the local garage and pile them as high as required to keep plants out of the reach of frost. If a pile of more than three tyres is needed, drive a stake down the space in the middle so that they do not fall over. Now fill the space with earth, decomposing compost, old hay or manure, if available; the decomposition is not essential but will provide added warmth. Plant your crops up top. Even fruit trees work with this method, as long as the tyres are well staked until the roots grow down below the level of the tyres. Water well: drainage can be too good in tyre gardens.

MANURE–HEATED PIT GARDENS
Dig a hole about 60 cm deep, pile in leaves or decomposing manure. Cover with sandy soil. Plant the vegetables. Now lay a few stakes over the pit and balance old windows or clear plastic on a few bricks so that they are oriented to the morning sun. This is called a cold frame.

These beds can also be used to help strike cuttings that need bottom heat or to get early seedlings for spring planting. The heat generated by the decomposing material should mean that the pit is relatively frost-free.

HEATED FROST-FRAME GARDENS

Make a manure or compost pile about 60 cm high. Lightly cover it with soil. Carefully fit a cold frame over the top of it, so that the top is level with the top of the pile and the main slope is oriented to the morning sun. A good mix for the compost pile is equal parts of coarse leaves (not gum leaves) and fresh cow or horse manure. This mixture produces a good, long-lasting heat. Experiment with any other compostable material on hand.

Wait about a week before planting out the cold frame to give the bed a chance to warm up evenly.

SOIL

My second garden was outside Canberra. It faced north, had a wonderful outlook, and good water from a nearby dam. It had everything, in fact, except good soil; instead, it had hard shale.

So we made our own soil. We carted litter from a nearby stable and piled it on top of the shale. We gathered weeds and sheep droppings and muck from the grocer and composted it or left it in heaps to rot. We didn't dig in any of the new soil; we let the earthworms and other soil life incorporate the new material naturally into the layers below. By the time we left two years later, we could dig down into the once hard crust of the hill and the carrots were able to dig their roots down, too.

If you have poor soil but do not want to bring in masses of new material, you can grow your own. Grow crops of 'green manure' — nitrogen-fixing crops such as broad beans, lupins, peas or even bulk-producing crops like sunflowers — they are fast-growing and decompose well as long as, like all crops grown for green manure, they are slashed just *before* they flower. Don't dig in the slashed plants; scatter with blood and bone or pelletised hen manure, clear a few rows down the middle, and grow more green manure. Keep going for three or four years, until there is soil instead of shale. This is lots of work, but one of the most rewarding experiences I know is to see concrete-like earth or yellow shale turn into soil.

If the garden slope is too great to allow green manure crops to be grown, try trees instead. Cut sloping channels across the hill, gradually easing downwards. When it rains, these will fill with silt and will catch moisture even in light showers. Plant trees along the channel; first of all, hardy ones like wattles or whatever will grow vigorously on poor disturbed soil. For stock feed, try tree lucerne instead. The new growth from both wattles and tree lucerne can be constantly pruned and left on the soil to decompose and turn into fertile loam.

If you live in a city or other polluted area (and country areas can be as bad or worse, especially near highways, or with aerial-spraying neighbours), some measures can be taken to minimise the effects of pollution.

• Grow barriers of tall trees, then shrubs to catch dust and other pollutants (as well as to stop noise).

• Hose down the shrubs every few days so that caught material falls to the ground. Do not grow edibles in the soil below.

• Maintain high levels of organic matter in the garden to 'fix' heavy metal pollutants and to break down others.

POLLUTION

In a heavily polluted area, plant barriers of trees and shrubs. Don't grow edible plants in soil that has been there for years, as it will have accumulated pollutants which may be passed on. Make above-ground gardens (see p. 27); bring in soil or organic matter for compost from elsewhere. Don't recycle nutrients from gardens in polluted areas; use garden refuse on ornamentals only and keep a separate compost bin of brought-in kitchen scraps and other scavenged material. Wash vegetables well before using, adding a little vinegar to the water.

A glasshouse or shade house will protect the garden from lead-bearing or other polluted dust. An old mosquito net above the garden will catch most of the dust without excess shading. Wash it every few days, away from the garden, and take it down before rain.

Use water filters if unsure of the purity of the water supply. Rainwater in city areas is likely to be more polluted than the tap water as roofs collect polluted dusts.

A garden designed to minimise the effects of pollution

SALT

Seaside gardens suffer from wind and salt. Treat salt as a pollutant and follow the advice for a polluted garden: barriers of trees and shrubs, mosquito net or shadecloth barrier, etc.

• Choose plants with hairy leaves or thin leaves which will probably withstand winds and drying. Plants with a high oil content in their leaves, such as lavender, are also suitable.

• Research what grew naturally in the area before it was cleared and plant those species as windbreaks.

• Build stone, brick or sleeper walls wherever possible. Walled gardens are the traditional safeguard against wind and salt. Make high walled courtyards for trees and shrubs and low walls above vegetable areas.

WEEDS

WEEDS AS SOIL IMPROVERS

Weeds are soil colonisers. They stabilise soil that has been disturbed; other plants can then germinate and grow. You can see this after bushfires or floods, when a crop of weeds gives way to saplings. Without these weeds the bare soil would erode in wind and rain, or compact to a seedling-resistant concrete.

Weeds often improve the soil they grow in. It is fascinating to compare the soil under old clumps of blackberries around this property with the soil in old paddocks. The blackberry-enriched soil is dark and fertile from years of dropped blackberry leaves and from deep roots bringing up nutrients that have leached deep down. Even bracken, with its nitrogen-fixing root bacteria, improves the soil it grows in, as do dock, broom and nettles.

Weeds are a natural form of green manuring, although other green manures (see p. 4) may be tidier and probably easier to manage than a crop of self-sown weeds. A few good piles of weeds every year are all the feeding most trees need. Most weeds make excellent compost (but beware of any which are covered in seeds, as the seeds may germinate). Cover seed-covered weeds with water and make pale brown liquid manure. The seeds will rot in the water so both the water and the seed-free sludge can be used.

We slash annual weeds in our vegetable areas, rather than pull them out. This prevents the weeds overshadowing the plants and it provides valuable mulch for the vegetables. Weeds flower more often when stimulated by the slashing; this attracts predators that may help control any pests. This method of weed control requires frequent slashing and fertile soil which can support a few weeds as well as the vegetables.

WEEDS, DISEASE AND PEST CONTROL

Many plants are less susceptible to disease if they are surrounded by weeds. There may be several reasons for this. Weeds may separate susceptible plants, blocking spores, etc. that may spread from infected plants to healthy ones. It is also possible that certain weeds, such as thistles and nettles, do give some resistance to disease. Plants grown with weeds often have fewer pests.

Conventional growing wisdom advises eradication of any weed that may harbour a crop-feeding pest. However, a year-round population of pests should also have a year-round population of predators to feed on them (predators cannot survive without a regular food supply). This means that when the season is right for a pest explosion, you can rely on a population of predators breeding up just behind. Several studies overseas show that various crops have fewer pests when the weeds are controlled rather than eradicated.

Weeds also disguise the other plants and pests find it harder to recognise the scent or shape of their preferred food. In addition, pests often actually prefer weeds to plants.

Unfortunately, weeds can also harbour disease, or pests such as aphids that spread disease from weeds to plants.

USEFUL WEEDS

BLACKBERRY
A wonderful soil conditioner and pest repellent which provides fruit and flowers for useful bird and insect predators. Slashing or mowing blackberry results in deep, black, leaf-rich soil afterwards. See also Blackberry, p. 31.

BRACKEN
This is another nitrogen-fixer, one of the first colonisers when soil is disturbed. It inhibits the growth and germination of many plants, including most grasses; on the other hand, trees do very well with it.

BROOM
Broom fixes nitrogen, repels pests and appears to give some protection against curly leaf in peaches and apple scab. Plant it around young trees to protect them from being eaten by wallabies.

DANDELION
A deep-rooted, traditional plant tonic. See Dock, below, for control.

DOCK
A lovely, deep-rooted weed which brings up nutrients that have leached down so deep in the soil that shallow-rooted vegetables cannot draw on them. When dock leaves return to the soil, the nutrients go back, too. Dock can be killed by stabbing it with a stake, then pouring a kettle full of boiling water down the hole.

NETTLE
Nettles are one of the traditional plant tonics; they are nitrogen-fixing and reputedly encourage earthworms. Nettle tea discourages fungal disease and helps increase frost resistance. Nettles also repel certain pests, especially sap-suckers. They hurt bare skin but are not a problem in an orchard where mostly long skirts, trousers or wellington boots are worn.

TEA TREE
Tea tree repels pests but can also stunt the growth of other plants. It is best kept just as a barrier around an orchard, not growing between the trees.

THISTLE
An insect repellent, but troublesome.

VETCH
This smothers other weeds that may not be so easily pulled out. It also inhibits the germination of many other weed seeds. Vetch itself is easily removed.

WANDERING JEW
This is a real pest in the flower or vegetable garden but makes quite a good cover under fruit trees, as long as it is regularly mown. Trees do far better with a cover of Wandering Jew than with grass underneath them (grass inhibits the growth of the small feeder roots of many trees). Slash and mow this weed often to keep it under reasonable control.

WEED CONTROL

Weeds are good companions to plants if they are not allowed to dominate the relationship.

• Don't remove what is already growing unless you are planting something else there immediately. This is the first rule for bush regeneration and applies to gardening also. As discussed, weeds condition the soil, increasing fertility and improving pest control. Try not to let a 'new' weed become entrenched in your garden, however.

• Instead of using overhead watering, drip irrigate flowers and vegetables. This waters only the plants, not the weeds.

• Keep weeds mown or whippersnippered so that they cannot go to seed. This will often control annual weeds and the debris can be used as mulch. (On the other hand, many perennial weeds may simply spread after mowing.)

• Compost weeds.

• Stick weeds in a drum, cover with water and make liquid manure and mulch.

• Let annual weeds that have not seeded wilt as mulch.

WEED-FREE GARDENS
Weeds are mostly found in unnatural cropping systems. Avoid:

• Repeated digging;

• Wide spacing between plants;

• High-nitrogen fertilisers; and

• Soil bare of leaf litter or mulch.

ABOVE-GROUND GARDEN BEDS
A garden built up with weed-free materials should stay relatively weed-free. The higher the garden bed is raised, the less likely weeds are to colonise it.

• Mow or slash grass and weeds, or jump up and down on them a few times until they are crushed. Do *not* put paper down as this stops the top layers of material from amalgamating with the soil and is unnecessary if there is sufficient green matter on top.

• Cover squashed weeds or grass with at least 30 cm of compost or wilted comfrey or lucerne hay, with a thinner layer of compost on top, or even good sterilised garden soil. Don't use 'first cut' lucerne which may have weed seeds in it. Alternatively, if hay contains weed seeds, shake it thoroughly or let the hens loose in it a few days before using. They will clean up most of the seeds.

• If hay or compost is unavailable, lay down a good layer of dead weeds, well-wilted and with seed heads cut off, then cover with 'pockets' of soil. Plant your seedlings in these and water and fertilise well; the weeds should quickly decompose to form more soil.

IN-GROUND WEED-FREE BEDS
Try the following:

Digging. Dig the ground, wait for weeds to germinate while watering well, then dig again three weeks after the first time.

Green manure. Plant a green manure crop as thickly as it will grow to choke out weeds. It will also provide humus and nutrients. I use sunflowers grown from cheap bird seed, slashed (before flowering) until tender and left on the ground as mulch. Buckwheat, available from health food stores, is a cheap, fast-growing green manure crop and an excellent weed choker which will grow on poor soil.

Clear plastic or solarisation. Dig, then cover the dug soil with clear plastic for three weeks. This encourages germination but the resultant weeds are short-lived as the heat under the plastic kills off young growth.

Covering. Cover the soil with mulch or a perforated weed mat, not black plastic, then plant seedlings in all or part of the mulch. If planting seedlings in mulch, douse them with chamomile tea to prevent damping off and add some nitrogen-rich material such as blood and bone or liquid manure to compensate for the nitrogen locked up as the mulch decomposes. It may not be necessary to add fertiliser to higher nutrient mulches, such as comfrey, compost, green lucerne or a leaf and grass clipping mixture.

Grazing. Sheep, pigs, hens, goats and caged rabbits will clean up weeds. Try temporary tethers, a small round fence made from reinforcing mesh, or electric fences.

KILLING WEEDS

Deep mulch. Many perennial weeds can also be controlled with mulch, applied thickly and regularly renewed. Often perennial weeds peep through mulch but by then they are loosely rooted and can be pulled out easily.

The vampire technique. For deep-rooted weeds such as dandelions and chicory, thrust a pointed stake into the heart of the plants. Now pour on boiling water.

Boiling water. A good dose of boiling water will kill most tender or shallow-rooted weeds. Repeat the dose if the weed appears again.

Companion planting. Mexican tradition plants melons with corn. The melons suppress the weeds and the fruit is a bonus. Plant crops as thickly as possible; bare ground invites weeds. Sweet potatoes planted with corn are another traditional weed-suppressant crop; try planting peas thickly with taller vegetables to provide a quick weed-suppressing, nitrogen-fixing soil cover.

The vampire technique

Natural herbicides. Many plants produce substances either in their roots or leaves that suppress the growth of other plants. This is described in greater detail in my book, *Guide to Companion Planting* (Aird Books). My favourite natural herbicides are the brassicas. Let cabbages, cauliflowers, etc. go to seed and then die off. They will 'sterilise' the ground around them, inhibiting germination and growth. Pull out the old plants, leave the ground bare for three weeks, then plant your crop.

Thickly planted sunflowers can also be used to inhibit weed growth. Thickly planted marigolds will inhibit couch grass, bindjis and various other weeds.

Ploughing with radishes. Scatter radish seed thickly on newly dug soil. Radishes will germinate and grow quickly, choking out weed competition. A month later, pull out the radishes and plant your new crop.

Drip irrigation. Use drip irrigation and water only the crops, which will then choke out the weeds.

Digging. A last resort technique, bad for human backs and soil.

Keep birds from your crops by feeding them with leftovers from the last harvest, or bird food bought cheaply in bulk.

To avoid powdery mildew on cucumbers and zucchini, trail the plants over the edges of the garden, as shown here, or grow them in vertical concrete pipes or tyre gardens.

Lerp psyllids may be disfiguring, but are usually controlled by predators, and cause little harm to the plant.

Tachinid flies pollinate plants and prey on a wide range of pests including borers.

TOLERATING WEEDS

Learn to live with weeds where possible. Give the crop an advantage so that it wins the battle for resources with the weeds; keep the crop growing strongly so that the weeds cannot compete. Weeds that grow after the first two-thirds of a crop's life will not affect the yield of the crop, although weeds that seed in that period may affect young plants in the crop to come. In many cases, weed control after the halfway point in a crop's life is wasted labour.

Weeds should be controlled as early as possible, before they can compete with crops and before they can seed or spread, and while little labour or other resources are needed to remove them. Many weeds, like couch grass, exude root toxins that inhibit the growth of other plants; the more the weeds grow, the less the crop is able to outstrip them.

If you have an area that is impossible to keep weed-free, don't try. Dig it up and plant as thickly as possible with marigolds, poppies, sunflowers, oats, rye, buckwheat or brassicas (and let them go to seed). These will inhibit weed germination and growth. Alternatively, try animal grazing (see p. 28).

LAWN WEEDS

Most lawn weeds can be controlled by regular mowing. Never let weeds seed, never mow so short that bare patches appear in the lawn to be colonised by weeds. Regular mowing will provide a thicker, more weed-resistant sward.

Sprinkle sulphate of ammonia on pale green patches of bindiis and water it in the next day. The grass should be more resistant to burning from the sulphate of ammonia and the bindiis will have borne the full brunt of it. You can use day-old undiluted urine instead of sulphate of ammonia. The added fertiliser will help the grass quickly fill up the bare patches. Don't worry if the grass dies off a little; it will soon come back, while the weeds won't. See Chapter Nine, Lawns.

PAVING WEEDS

• Make sure material used under paving is weed-free.

• Water thoroughly and pull weeds out.

• Chip weeds out with a spade.

• Whip weeds out with a whippersnipper; this will have to be repeated but with practice is as easy as mowing the lawn.

• Sprinkle with borax. Warning: this will kill all plant life around.

• Paint weeds with kerosene.

• Plant paving crevices with desirable plants, like thyme or chamomile.

Remember: any bare ground is unstable and will be recolonised, probably by weeds.

SOME STUBBORN WEEDS

BINDII
See Lawns, p. 136.

BRACKEN
Get rid of bracken unless you are regenerating an area with trees. Leaf drip from bracken fronds contains phenolic compounds which suppress the growth of various grains, grasses and trees. Use it for mulch or in compost instead; bracken is high in potash. Bracken will not stand repeated cutting. Mow it whenever new fronds appear. This may mean mowing every three weeks to be effective. If the young fronds are allowed to harden they will start renewing the root reserves, instead of depleting them. Half-hearted mowing will just mean a healthier crop of young bracken.

Even more effective is bending or bruising the fronds. This means that the plant exhausts itself trying to repair repeatedly damaged fronds. An old wire bed frame dragged along the ground will wound large areas of bracken; done every few weeks during the growing season, this should diminish the bracken considerably. In small areas, mow or use a brush cutter. If bracken is mown as often as grass, the area will be bracken-free within one season.

Close and heavy-footed grazing also works, but bracken can be toxic to stock. Lots of persistent, scratching hens will eradicate bracken.

COUCH

Cover couch in early spring with newspaper, black plastic or mulch at least 20 cm thick. In larger areas plough and weed, plough and weed. It takes about two years to get rid of couch this way. Covering with even a thin layer of mulch helps because the couch is then easier to pull out. A thick planting of marigolds will choke out couch (the leaves and roots produce a substance that inhibits its growth) as will a thickly planted crop of brassicas left to go to seed. Grown very thickly, sunflowers will inhibit (but not eradicate) couch.

A good soaking with boiling water will get rid of couch; this is only suitable for small patches in the garden. Try scattering sulphate of ammonia thickly on dry couch. Leave for three days before watering. The couch below will be dead and a good watering will spread the sulphate of ammonia so it turns into fertiliser, not herbicide. Do the same with three-day-old undiluted urine (old urine turns ammoniacal and ammonia kills the grass).

Keep couch out of the garden with a barrier of thickly planted comfrey, or lemon grass, or even dahlias. Brick, stone or wooden walls will assist.

DANDELION

Stab with a wooden stake then pour boiling water down the hole.

OXALIS, ONION WEED, NUT GRASS

Dig these during early spring or late winter, at old bulb exhaustion stage, just as they start to make new growth. Dig to a fork-depth and carefully shake out the soil so that the roots are not broken from the bulblets. Dig them out repeatedly at this stage and with luck any bulblets left will be too small to survive.

Oxalis usually only grows where there is insufficient grass competition: on steep banks or under trees. My favourite way to get rid of oxalis is to plant a daisy, lavender or some other fast-growing cutting. In two years the weed will be buried under the daisy or lavender bush.

PATERSON'S CURSE

Mow repeatedly at 'rosette' stage, just before flowering, until it loses vigour, then plough and graze it heavily with sheep. *Never* let Paterson's curse flower; one plant can seed four square metres and it flowers incessantly.

RAGWORT

Bruise the plants with your boots or slash; try sprinkling with half a cup of sulphate of potash.

SORREL

Good garden care will gradually get rid of sorrel; organic matter reduces the acidity and aerates the soil. Mulch and add a little dolomite each season until the sorrel vanishes.

SUMMER GRASS OR CRAB GRASS

This is an annual. Mow regularly in spring before it sets seed and it should disappear. If necessary, mow your neighbour's lawn too. This will be cheaper and more pleasant than using herbicide.

THISTLES

Overgrazing brings thistles. Behead them just before they flower, or mow them and rake them up for a high-silica compost or green manure spray. Grass inhibits thistle germination. Stop grazing until a good grass cover grows again, or resow pasture. Thistles are a sign of bad grass management. Once the grass is doing well, the thistles will disappear.

LARGE-SCALE WEED CONTROL: BLACKBERRY

Blackberries mostly grow on disturbed land that often benefits from the stability of blackberry roots and cover. Old farm land in particular is prone to blackberry infestation.

Around here blackberries grow mostly on old abandoned mullock heaps, but they also spread out into land disturbed for orchards and onto pasture land, where the land has been overgrazed or overcleared and tends to 'slump' or erode after heavy rain. Those slumps usually host blackberries next season. The blackberries grow well, up to three metres high, spreading out up to one metre each season.

Slowly, however, trees will start to emerge from the clumps. Here they are mostly *Pittosporum undulatum*, a rainforest fringe species that germinates in the warm, moist, damp blackberry clumps and grows tall and spindly until it reaches the top of the blackberries, then branches out, gradually covering the blackberry clump until it dwindles to a few canes, starved of light and moisture. Pittosporums seem particularly effective at choking out blackberries (they also have root secretions that inhibit the growth of plants nearby).

Black wattles may also assist, and bananas, passionfruit, chokos or even pumpkins can be grown over the clumps to limit blackberry growth.

The fastest blackberry control is done with a bulldozer or tractor with a front-end loader. The blackberries are simply uprooted, pushed into a heap and burnt. This is quick and effective as long as grass (or something else) is sown immediately in the bare patches.

Burning will work if the fire is hot enough to destroy most of the blackberry bush. This may mean using flame guns or a spray of diesel if the clumps are in a damp place, as blackberries often are. Again, as soon as the blackberries are burnt, a cover of grass must be planted. Follow-up is needed through the season, digging up new blackberry shoots.

Animal grazing can also have magical success. Some friends have cleared most of their creek flats with tethered goats, moving them every few days, slashing down blackberries for them to reach, then sowing grass as the goats are moved to another area that needs clearing. The result is lovely loam, enriched with years of blackberry leaves and goat droppings.

An old neighbour had a faster blackberry control technique; he circled each clump with an electric fence and put in some pigs and a bag of pig nuts strewn over the clumps. By the time the pigs had finished rooting for the nuts the blackberries were finished, too. Wallabies, horses and sheep will eat young blackberry shoots, as will other animals.

Small clumps of blackberries near the house can be ignored or, even better, mown.

There is no single infallible organic technique for getting rid of blackberries. All techniques require follow-up and dedication. Blackberry control has to become part of an ongoing management plan.

ORGANIC REMEDIES

No matter how good the growing system is, factors such as unseasonal weather conditions and the introduction of pests (as a result of a lack of predators or a general pest/predator imbalance from pesticides used nearby) may all cause problems in the garden.

The methods below should be used as temporary measures while you identify and remedy the problem. (In most cases, better feeding and more predator attractants will be the answer.) Organic sprays break down quickly and cause the least possible harm to the environment, including humans. Even so, use them only as a last resort. *Any* spraying, organic or not, may kill predators and even sprays that are 'target-specific' (killing a particular pest) remove predators' food supply, causing them either to die or to move on. A good organic garden always has a few pests and a small population of predators, ready to build up in response to any increase in pest numbers.

Always remember that the best way to control pests is to have healthy soil, constant blossom and other features that attract predators.

BEFORE SPRAYING, TRY:
• Waiting a week or so. See if pest numbers start to decline naturally.

• Mechanical methods. Pick off pests by hand, use a strong hose, dust off with a paint brush (aphids especially).

• Traps. These include cardboard wrapped round trees to trap codling moth; port wine or pheromone lures; light traps (these usually suppress egg laying); yellow painted boards; aphid traps, made from ice-cream containers of water with yellow colouring and detergent; molasses and water grasshopper traps.

Aphid trap

• Barriers. These include grease-bands to deter ants; trenches filled with derris-impregnated straw to deter cutworms, or try toothpick stakes around seedlings; wood ash to keep away slugs; nets to keep out birds; mesh screen or pantyhose to keep away codling moth or cabbage white butterflies and moths.

Cutworm trench

• Tricks. These include interplanting.

• Repellents. Bordeaux keeps away cabbage white butterflies, slugs and snails; garlic spray keeps away aphids and cabbage white butterflies; tansy spray keeps away cabbage white butterflies and cabbage moth; try mint, onion and chilli sprays; reflective mulch repels aphids and thrips; green hessian sacking deters cabbage white butterflies and cabbage moths.

• Predator lures. Pollen or Marmite sprays smeared on plants will attract hoverflies, lacewings, etc.

HOW TO USE ORGANIC REMEDIES

• Label any pesticide **POISON** and **KEEP OUT OF REACH OF CHILDREN**. Use at once if possible. Remember that many organic remedies are poisonous not only to the pests they are intended for, but also to beneficial organisms such as bees and lacewings, and sometimes to humans, too. Treat all pesticides and fungicides as dangerous unless you are sure that they are not.

• When spraying a large number of trees or plants, always spray every second plant or every second row, then spray the rest a week later. This method of spraying will ensure some of the pests and predators survive.

• Reapply pesticides when necessary. Organic pesticides break down quickly and plants may become reinfested. Organic remedies must be used more frequently than conventional controls. No control is worth much without a change in the growing methods.

• Be ruthless. If a plant is continually diseased or pest-prone it may be a poor cultivar or unsuited to the area. Do not persevere with such plants. Keep seed from well-adapted plants, take cuttings from neighbours' gardens and where possible avoid greenhouse-grown plants from other regions.

HOW TO CHECK FOR PESTS

Always look under leaves as well as on top; examine the trunk just below soil level as well as above it; breathe on flower petals, so thrips move.

Natural markings tend to be evenly distributed (like the spores under fern fronds, which can be mistaken for scale pests). Pests and diseases seem to come in blobs and blotches. If a marking is raised above the leaf or fruit, however, it is probably a pest or disease. Do not treat a pest or disease unless it is harming the plant beyond endurance.

SYMPTOM SORTER

Many of the remedies given can be used for more than one pest or disease. If a pest is difficult to identify, try to identify the exact damage it is causing and treat it by the symptoms. If the pest seems to be sucking sap, if leaves are mottled or new shoots wilt, try the remedies suggested for aphids or red spider mite. If leaves are chewed, look up caterpillars or beetles or bugs. If the damage is critical, mix up a pyrethrum spray with chamomile tea and seaweed spray. Spray in the evening, under the leaves as well as on top, and then try to identify the problem so that specific action can be taken.

BORERS

Symptoms: Shoots and even branches may die back; look for holes and sawdust deposits.
Control: Poke out borers with wire; plug up holes; inject derris or pyrethrum.

FUNGAL AND BACTERIAL PROBLEMS

Symptoms: Leaf spots or blemishes; fruit rots.
Control: Spray Bordeaux on old tough foliage (not blossom or new shoots) or dormant trees; use chamomile, elder, chive or horseradish or seaweed sprays as preventives.

LEAF EATERS

Common pests: Earwigs, grasshoppers, caterpillars, leaf-eating ladybirds.
Symptoms: Holes in leaves, ragged leaves, large green droppings.
Control: Encourage birds; pick off by hand or hose off; sprinkle on dried wood ash, diatomaceous earth or lime (be careful not to overlime the soil); spray them with pikelet spray; use Bordeaux or other repellent sprays; use wormwood, tomato leaf sprays or bug juice; derris spray (spray underneath the leaves as well) or pyrethrum.

NUTRITIONAL PROBLEMS

Symptoms: Foliage yellows, on either young or old leaves or between veins; plants are stunted, crops are small and may drop off before maturity.
Control: The best food for plants is plant and animal matter. Compost and mulch should be all the feeding plants need. If in doubt give plants a daily dose of liquid foliar fertiliser for a couple of weeks. If the plants improve, keep doing it once a week or fortnight while the feeding program is corrected.

ROOT ROTS

Symptoms: Plants yellow or die back suddenly, usually from the top; plants will rock unsteadily when shaken.
Control: By the time symptoms are visible, fatal damage has usually been done. Try to correct the underlying cause, i.e. poor drainage, so that future plantings do not suffer the same fate. If the victim is a tree, try cutting it back as a temporary measure and feed it with foliar spray while mulching with compost and correcting the drainage. It may be better to dig out the tree in order to stop the rot spreading to other plants.

SAP-SUCKERS

Common pests: Aphids, bugs, cicadas, scale, thrips, mites, leafhoppers.
Symptoms: Skeletonised foliage; foliage is brown or curled at the edges; leaves appear mottled or pitted. Sap-suckers may also damage new shoots; shoots wilt and die off suddenly. Sap-suckers excrete a lot of sugary wastes which in turn can promote sooty mould and a procession of ants feeding on the sugary excreta.
Control: Encourage birds and other predators; use oil sprays in temperatures below 20°C, soap sprays in temperatures above 24°C; try rhubarb, garlic, nettle, quassia, derris or wormwood sprays.

OTHER SYMPTOMS

DIEBACK

This can be caused by insect attack, so check if the leaf edges are ragged or the stems chewed. Dieback can also be caused by root rots. It may be caused by borers; look for holes and sawdust deposits. Sap-suckers may cause dieback; see if the young shoots are dying back first. Sometimes dieback from sap-suckers on new shoots will spread as a pathogen enters the injury.

FAILURE TO GROW

• Plants which have been badly treated in the past may take several years to start to grow again. If a new tree is not growing, always check for root rot, which may have been imported with the tree. Root rots are best dug out before they spread.

- Check that plants are adequately fed and watered and are not suffering through competition with grass or larger plants. Old gardens and orchards may suffer from 'replant disease'; new plants grown where old ones have been often will not thrive, possibly due to a gradual build-up of soil pathogens and soil deficiencies to which the older plants had developed a tolerance. Gradually improve the soil condition using mulch and compost and you will eventually solve this.

- Look for scale. Scale injects substances that stop plants growing.

- Plants may also be stunted by leaking gas mains. Sniff for leaks in still weather.

- Plants will not thrive in areas that are too cold or too hot. Measures such as shading pergolas, ice on the roots, hessian shelters, etc. may partially solve the problem but in most cases it will not be worth the trouble. There are so many species now available in Australia, for climates ranging from cold to tropical, that it is more sensible to keep to climatic limitations.

LACK OF FRUIT

Young trees may not set fruit or it may fall off before ripe. Frost and hail can damage young fruit or destroy blossom so that it falls before fruit set. Try to remember if there was frost, strong wind or hail at blossoming time. Brown rot can also damage blossom.

Many fruit trees need a pollinator to set fruit. An apple tree may have fruited by itself for years, but if the neighbouring pollinator (perhaps several houses away) has been recently cut down, the result will be no fruit. Poor pollination may result in no fruit setting or premature fruit drop. Cut open a fallen fruit. If it has no, few or misshapen seeds, there is probably a pollination problem. Plant flowers and flowering shrubs to attract bees at the same time that the trees flower.

Codling moth and fruit fly larvae damage the seeds; the fruit then falls prematurely. See pp. 51–53 and pp. 53–56.

LEAF FALL

Check that the plant is not waterlogged or starved of water, has been adequately fed, and is not being overshadowed by a taller tree or bush. One of the most common questions from Canberra gardeners is, 'Why has my lemon tree lost its leaves?' The answer is usually low temperatures. Cold-stressed plants don't always look black and frostbitten. Cold-stressed citrus may simply turn listless, yellow and finally defoliate. Another reason for leaf fall can be the old age of those particular leaves. Don't worry as long as no young or middle-aged leaves are falling.

YELLOWING LEAVES

If the oldest leaves are yellowing but the young ones aren't, the plant has a nitrogen deficiency. If the young leaves are yellowing the plant may have a phosphorous deficiency. If all leaves are yellowing evenly, check that the plant is not waterlogged or starved of water. Cold weather or herbicide drift will cause yellowing. Check the base of the plant for collar rot or injury from a lawnmower.

PESTICIDES

BORDEAUX SPRAY

See Fungicides, pp. 40–41 for recipe. This is effective against scale and to a lesser extent mites. It repels slugs, snails, borers and many other pests.

BUG JUICE

Try this on any pest. Success will be variable, but bug juice *can* be so effective that no other remedy will be required. Take 1 part pest, add

3 parts water. Blend. Leave in a warm (not hot) place for 24 hours. Strain. Dilute with 50 parts water.

Bug juice may work because. of pathogens or parasites on the pests, or because the odour is unpleasant to the other pests, or even both.

BUTTERMILK SPRAY

Use for red spider mites and other mites, as well as their eggs. Mix ½ cup buttermilk, 4 cups flour and 50 cups water. Spray every two days, under as well as on top of the foliage.

CHILLI SPRAY

A repellent spray for anything that eats or sucks leaves. It may also kill caterpillars and other soft- and sensitive-bodied pests. Take 1 cup chopped chillies or 1 cup chilli sauce or Tabasco sauce. Add an equal quantity of water, leave overnight, strain and spray.

CLAY SPRAY

This will suffocate aphids, thrips and mites. It will also work for scale, but use clay, not soil, or you may make your scale problem worse. Dilute some clay with enough water to make it sprayable. Be careful not to spray on predators such as ladybird larvae, as it will kill them, too.

CORIANDER SPRAY

This is effective against red spider mites and woolly aphids. Boil 1 part coriander leaves in 1 part water for 10 minutes. Strain and spray. This can also be used with anise. Alternatively, mix 4 parts coriander oil in 100 parts soapy water. Shake well until mixed.

DERRIS SPRAY

A useful general insecticide, Derris works best when eaten. It is effective on leaf eaters such as caterpillars and pear and cherry slugs, sap-suckers such as aphids, and most weevils, spitfires and fleas. Derris causes minimal harm to humans, but will kill fish (including goldfish), tadpoles, frogs, toads and various ladybird larvae, but not hoverfly larvae or bees.

Derris breaks down in sunlight after a few days but is longer lasting than pyrethrum.

Derris powder is more conveniently used in spray form. Mix 120 g soap in 4.5 L water. Add 60 g derris powder mixed in another 4.5 L water. Dilute with 12 L water, mix again and spray. Remix if the spray separates. A simpler recipe: Mix 2 kg derris powder with 1 kg pure soap powder. Mix with 20 L water.

DIATOMACEOUS EARTH SPRAY

Use this against soft-bodied pests such as aphids, thrips, mites, snails and termites or hard-shelled pests such as bugs. The fine dust should penetrate their carapaces and gradually wear them away. Spray once every 2 weeks.

Mix 200 g diatomaceous earth (the finely ground skeletons of marine organisms) with 1 L soapy water.

DIPEL (*BACILLUS THURINGIENSIS*)

This is a biological control, a form of germ warfare. Dipel was a silkworm disease in Japan and a disease of wax moth larvae. It needs to be eaten to be effective. The spores are killed by sunlight and must be reapplied once a week. Spray under the leaves as well as on top.

Bacillus thuringiensis is effective on all moth or butterfly caterpillars. It is sometimes effective on sawfly larvae. The infected caterpillars may be eaten without harm by birds or any other predators. There have been no reports of caterpillar resistance to Dipel in Australia although there have been rumours of this overseas.

Use Dipel to make your own culture. Gather 1 cup of caterpillars from an area that has been sprayed with Dipel four days earlier. Mash them up and place in 3 cups warm milk. Cover and leave in a warm (not hot) place for three days. Strain, add 8 cups water, then spray. A little of the milk mixture can be saved as a starter for the next lot, or you can gather more infected caterpillars.

ELDER SPRAY

This is a general pest killer, particularly effective on aphids and caterpillars. It is also poisonous to humans and hoverfly larvae, although it appears to spare adult hoverflies, bees, ladybirds and ladybird larvae and most wasps.

Take 500 g elder leaves and smooth-barked stems and cover with 3.5 L water. Simmer for half an hour, topping up as the water boils away. Strain and use undiluted. Elder spray will keep for three months in a sealed container in a dark, cool place but keep out of the reach of children and label **POISON**. Elder spray can also be used as a fungicide.

EUCALYPTUS OIL SPRAY

Like other oils, eucalyptus oil kills scale, aphids, etc. You can substitute it for the oil spray below with even more effect. Use it only in cool weather or it may damage young leaves and flowers. Eucalyptus oil will also repel many pests.

GARLIC SPRAY

Use this as a general insecticide in a wide range of situations. Its effect is variable. Harsh, arid conditions make it possibly less effective. Remember, it is not a contact poison.

Chop 85 g unpeeled garlic and soak in 2 tablespoons mineral oil for 24 hours. Add 600 ml water in which 7 g soap has been dissolved (as soapy a solution as possible). Strain and store in glass, not metal, away from light. To 1 part of the base mixture, add 10 parts water. Strengthen as required by adding more base.

GLUE SPRAY

This will dry on small pests, suffocating them. Use on aphids, scale, mites, pear and cherry slugs and thrips. Spray every five to seven days. It is no use in wet weather.

Dissolve 1 cup glue in 3 cups warm water. Some glues are denser than others, so more water may be required. A home-made flour and water paste can also be used.

INSECT REPELLENT SPRAY

Blend a mixture of as many as possible of the following: garlic, chilli, horseradish, nettles, onion, lavender leaves or flowers, mints and yarrow. Use just enough water to ensure even blending. Let stand for 24 hours at room temperature in a closed container. Filter, add a few drops of detergent to help sticking, add an equal quantity of water and spray onto plants.

LANTANA SPRAY

This is effective against aphids. Boil 500 g leaves in 1 L water. Strain and spray. Lantana is a well known and troublesome weed, so do not plant it for the purpose of aphid control.

MARIGOLD SPRAY

This repels most sap-suckers and will kill aphids. Cover marigold flowers with boiling soapy water, leave overnight, strain and spray.

MELIA (CAPE LILAC) SPRAY

This kills snails and other soft-bodied pests, and any leaf-eating pest that eats foliage that has been sprayed with it. Place 1 cup chopped melia leaves in a jar. Cover with boiling water. Replace the lid. When cool, strain and spray. It is mildly toxic, so wear a mask and do not inhale the spray. Spray every three or four days if necessary for continued control. It breaks down quickly and should not be stored.

MUSTARD SPRAY

This kills scale. It is also an effective repellent spray, and has some fungicidal properties.

Mix powdered mustard seed with enough water to make a sprayable mixture. Most powdered table mustard is mixed with flour and turmeric. This can be used but will not be as strong as powdered pure mustard.

OIL SPRAY

Oil spray works by covering insects or their eggs with a light film of suffocating oil. It is especially effective in winter when the outsides of the insects or eggs are more porous. Oil spray causes leaf damage when the temperature is above 24°C.

Take 1 kg soap for every 8 L oil. Boil and stir vigorously until dissolved. Dilute with 20 times the volume of water. This spray separates quickly; do not store once it has been mixed with water.

ONION SPRAY

This is effective against scale, thrips, aphids and mites. Pour 500 g boiling water over 1 kg unpeeled, chopped onions and strain. Dilute with 20 L water. Spray every ten days until pests are gone.

ONION GARLIC SPRAY

This is effective for leaf-eating insects such as caterpillars, sap-suckers such as aphids, thrips and mites, but has a limited effectiveness on most scale and hard-surfaced pests such as shield bugs.

Chop 4 hot chillies, 4 large onions and 2 bulbs of garlic. Cover with soapy water and leave for 24 hours. Strain, add 2 L water and spray. Store in a sealed container in a dark place for up to two weeks if necessary.

PEPPER

Dust white or black pepper over caterpillars.

PIKELET SPRAY

This is my favourite spray. Take 1 cup white flour. Add 1 cup milk and mix well. (At this stage, eggs can be added to make pikelets for human consumption.) Add 5 cups water (delete for pikelets). Mix again and spray. The spray will dry to a milk-like lacquer and look horrible, but will wash off with the first rain shower or good hosing. By then the pests will be dead, suffocated by flour and milk. With luck the birds will decide they prefer batter-covered pests, and look for more pests to eat.

POWDERED SULPHUR

This is an old-fashioned mite remedy which also kills predators. It should not be used in hot weather, as plants may be burnt. Ask for powdered sulphur or flowers of sulphur at hardware stores or chemists.

PYRETHRUM SPRAY

Pyrethrum is a broad-spectrum spray, worth trying on any pests. It has a low toxicity for humans and other mammals but will kill some predators. One of the great organic gardening standbys, pyrethrum spray is easily made.

Pyrethrum (*Tanacetum cinerariifolium*) is a pretty, low-growing, grey-leafed herb with white-petalled daisy-like spring flowers round a yellow centre. *T. coccineum*, a red-flowered pyrethrum, also has insecticidal properties. Pyrethrum seed can be sown at any temperate time of the year, or large clumps can be divided in autumn. The low-growing plants need full sun, excellent drainage and reasonably fertile soil and moisture for good flowering. Keep pyrethrum free of weeds as it is prone to a range of fungal problems and overcrowding can make these worse. As pyrethrum gets older it is more susceptible to frost or fungal damage; plants usually do not survive for more than about five years.

Pyrethrum flowers should be picked when they have just opened, early in the morning. The main active ingredients are in the immature seeds. Pyrethrum flowers should be dried in a dark, well-ventilated place and stored in a dark place, as they lose their potency on contact with light.

The active ingredients in pyrethrum flowers are relatively insoluble in water, although a low potency spray can be made by covering the flowers with boiling water, leaving them to steep and spraying as soon as the mixture is cool. A much more effective spray is made by covering the flowers with kerosene, mineral oil or alcohol (brandy works well) and leaving overnight in a dark place, then adding 6 parts of water for 1 part of strained liquid. Use at once.

Pyrethrum breaks down in sunlight over a

period of anywhere from 2 hours to two days. Spray it outdoors at night so that it does not affect bees and other useful species. It has about a 12-hour toxicity.

Allergic reactions to pyrethrum include dermatitis, asthma and sinus problems.

QUASSIA SPRAY

Quassia is a general insecticide and a bird repellent for fruit. Use quassia for aphids, mites, caterpillars, sawfly larvae and pear and cherry slug. It is also worth experimenting with quassia on other soft-bodied pests. Quassia is harmless to nearly all predators and to bees. It contains quassin, a lactone with a very bitter taste, hence its value as a bird repellent as long as it does not rain. Quassia chips can be bought from organic suppliers.

Simmer 30 g quassia chips in 1 L water for one hour. Add more water as it evaporates. The liquid should be yellow. Strain, mix in enough soft soap to form a lather (about 30 g) and dilute with 5 parts water for aphids or 3 parts for sawfly larvae, pear and cherry slug, or mites like red spider mite.

To make a quassia infusion, steep 30 g quassia chips in 570 ml cold water for 2 hours, then strain and use.

RYANIA SPRAY

Ryania is a shrub native to Trinidad, cultivated in Latin America. It is very successful overseas against a wide range of caterpillars and beetles, including codling moth, but is less effective in the hotter, more arid Australian conditions. Ryania spray is also difficult to find in Australia and usually expensive. Ryania is harmless to most but not all common predators.

Mix 1 kg ryania powder with 100 L soapy water. Spray every ten to fourteen days.

SOAP SPRAY

Use soap made with caustic potash, not caustic soda (at least one variety is available from garden centres). Ordinary soap is far less effective and worse for the soil and plants. Do not use detergents.

Soap spray spares nearly all predators, as well as bees, but kills aphids, scale and small caterpillars. It penetrates insects' waxy cuticle and kills them. Mix the soap with water until milky and frothy. The amount needed will depend on the water hardness.

STINGING NETTLE SPRAY

Cover nettles with water and leave for three weeks, or until the liquid is pale brown to green. This can be diluted with 2 parts water and used for aphids. It is also a valuable foliar fertiliser and an excellent plant tonic; use freely.

STINK BUG SPRAY

This repels almost everything (including humans). It also kills most pests, including snails.

Fill a jar with stink bugs (use gloves to collect them). Cover with boiling water and replace the lid tightly. Leave for 24 hours. Strain and spray.

SUGAR SPRAY

Dissolve 2 kg sugar in a bucket of water. Drench the soil to kill nematodes. Molasses can also be used, but do not use honey, as it may transmit diseases to bees.

TANSY SPRAY

This is an excellent spray as long as it is washed off thoroughly before using the plant. It will not kill predators. Tansy spray is an antifeedant; it repels pests and inhibits their feeding rather than killing them. As it breaks down quite quickly, use tansy spray every two or three days.

Place 1 cup tansy in jar, cover with 1 cup boiling water. Put the lid on at once and do not sniff the steam. When the liquid is cool, strain and spray. Tansy spray can be stored for several days in a cool dark place. Keep it out of reach of children and mark it **POISON**.

WORMWOOD SPRAY

Wormwood is a bitter aromatic herb containing a volatile oil made up of various organic acids and glucoside absinthe. Wormwood's active ingredients come from its leaves and flowerheads, both of which can be used. Pick the leaves and flower stalks just before or during flowering for best effect, though they can be picked at any other time.

Wormwood spray both repels and kills fleas and other pests such as flies, moths and mosquitoes. It is effective against aphids and deters snails if sprayed around seedlings. Wormwood tea is an excellent insecticide for sap-suckers such as bean, tomato and onion fly and whitefly.

To make wormwood spray, cover chopped leaves with boiling water and leave for three hours. Dilute 1 part spray in 4 parts water.

FUNGAL AND BACTERIAL CONDITIONS

PREVENTION

• Avoid introducing disease. Mildew spores can be spread by wide skirts or brushing trousers. Bacterial gummosis can be spread on pruning tools.

• Keep plants healthy; they are less susceptible to disease.

• Try crop rotation as most diseases have specific hosts.

• Mulch frequently; this may cover infected material. I deep-mulch fruit trees and roses in winter, covering any diseased leaves. Mulch can also inhibit various pathogens. Verticulum wilt on potatoes or tomatoes, for example, can be inhibited with a barley straw mulch. *Phytophthora cinnamomi* is inhibited by a compost of lucerne hay and composted wattle

bark. Plants with mycorrhizal infection (which needs a stable and rich humus level) are less prone to fungal and bacterial infection.

• Use barrier crops. Barriers will inhibit the spread of disease spores by wind.

• Practise rigorous garden hygiene. Remove and burn infected fruit or leaves and prune out dead wood and twigs.

• Green manure assists crop rotation and inhibits some disease. A soybean green manure, for example, inhibits the build-up of potato scab.

• Improve air flow by pruning, thinning fruit or cutting air channels through the garden.

• Use liquid compost (see p. 15), seaweed, nettle, casuarina or horsetail sprays when required as preventives.

FUNGICIDES

ALL-PURPOSE PREVENTIVE SPRAY

Take as many of the following as possible: nettles, comfrey, chamomile, seaweed, waterweed, lucerne, yarrow, casuarina, horsetail and horseradish leaves. Cover with water. Spray on foliage when the water is weak tea colour. Add more water to the mixture and use again when strong enough. The remnant can finally be used for mulch.

BAKING SODA SPRAY

This is not strictly organic. Use instead of Bordeaux; it is slightly easier to make. Never use on foliage. Mix 100 g washing soda with 50 g soft soap. Dilute with 2 L water.

BORDEAUX MIXTURE

Bordeaux, the standard organic fungicide, is very effective against a wide range of parasitic fungi and bacteria. Pathogens do not seem to develop resistance to it as they do to many modern fungicides. Bordeaux sticks very strongly to trees once sprayed. If it has been made properly and used fresh, even rain should not affect it.

Always make Bordeaux mixture yourself. (Commercial mixtures are not traditional Bordeaux.) Use Bordeaux within one hour of making, or it will start to separate; after this, it won't stick to the plants and may injure them.

Try other, 'softer' fungicides before Bordeaux. It contains copper sulphate and too much copper can affect soil fungi (high humus levels can mitigate this), possibly killing predators. Try spraying every second bush, then spraying the rest ten days later so that predators are still present when pests start to build up.

Bordeaux is made from copper sulphate (bluestone) and calcium hydroxide (hydrated, bricky's or builder's lime.) Both can be bought from hardware stores. Agricultural lime, the sort usually used in the garden, does not work. Fine crystals of copper sulphate dissolve more easily than the coarse ones.

Ensure the hydrated lime is from an unopened bag. Once the calcium hydroxide is exposed to air, it becomes carbonated (i.e. turns into calcium carbonate) and will not neutralise the copper sulphate. The resulting spray may damage trees severely.

Mix 90 g blue copper sulphate with 6.5 L cold water in a non-metallic container: plastic, glass, wood or earthenware. Never use iron or galvanised iron for Bordeaux. In a second non-metallic container mix 125 g calcium hydroxide in another 2.5 L cold water. If either mixture is lumpy, strain it. Lime sometimes includes some sand and, unless strained, it may block the spray nozzle. The copper sulphate must be thoroughly dissolved or it may form a suspended precipitate that will sink to the bottom and not stick so well to the plants. Mix the two together. Stir well.

Test with an old nail; dip it in the mixture for 30 seconds. If it comes out blue, more lime is required, or more mixing to dissolve the lime. Do not use the mixture until the problem is corrected or it may burn plants.

Apply Bordeaux with any spraying equipment, and wash out the nozzles with water to stop them clogging. Bordeaux is used mostly at bud-swell for deciduous plants, after blossoming for evergreens and at half-strength on grapes and vegetables throughout the season for downy mildew.

When spraying trees, spray all the bark, including the crotch of the tree. If trees are prone to canker or branch dieback spray Bordeaux just before pruning. All the remaining leaves will drop off, so spray again after pruning, as infection may still enter at the new, uncovered places.

Large-scale recipe: For spraying large orchards, the conventional measure is 1 kg copper sulphate, 750 g lime to 100 L water. This is a slightly stronger recipe than above, but should be made and used in the same way.

BORDEAUX PASTE

This is useful for collar rot and tree wounds. Dissolve 60 g copper sulphate in 2 L water, then add 120 g bricky's lime also mixed in 2 L water. A tablespoon of powdered skim milk can also be added to increase effectiveness.

CONDY'S CRYSTALS

Use this for powdery mildew. Dissolve 7 g potassium permanganate (Condy's crystals) in 7 L water. Spray at once.

GARLIC SPRAY

See p. 37, Pesticides. Garlic spray is an effective fungicide; unfortunately it also kills insects, so should be used with discretion. Use garlic spray for brown rot, curly leaf and fusarium wilt.

CHAMOMILE TEA

This is a very mild fungicide. Cover a handful of flowers in boiling water or use a teabag, following instructions on the packet. Spray when cool. Chamomile tea is excellent for damping off (drizzle round seedlings); or for spraying on fruit every few days to ward off brown rot.

CHIVE TEA

Chive tea is made the same way as chamomile tea and used for the same purposes. It is especially good against apple scab, and should be sprayed every two weeks in the last months of winter until just before bud-swell.

HORSERADISH SPRAY

This can be used for brown rot and curly leaf. Take 1 cup leaves, cover with water and boil, covered, for 20 minutes. Add 4 parts water to 1 part horseradish liquid. Spray at once.

MILK SPRAY

This is effective against a range of mildews. Spray equal parts of milk and water every few days until the condition is cleared.

MUSTARD SEED FLOUR

Grind mustard seeds to a fine powder. Dust over plants affected by powdery mildew.

NETTLE TEA

This can be used against powdery mildew. It is also effective against aphids. Take a container of nettles, cover with water and leave for three weeks, or until the water is mid-brown. Spray undiluted.

SEAWEED SPRAY

This should be sprayed throughout the year at monthly intervals to combat brown rot, curly leaf, black spot and other fungal and bacterial conditions. Spray on foliage at any time of the year; it will also act as a foliar fertiliser and help increase frost resistance.

Wash seaweed if it has been exposed to salt spray on the beach. Weed fresh from the sea needs no washing. Cover with water, leave until the water turns pale brown and spray. To reuse, add more water to the residue. The remaining organic matter can finally be used as an excellent weed-free mulch.

URINE

Human urine is very effective against apple and pear scab and a range of mildews. Fresh urine is sterile, unless the donor has a urinary tract infection, but does not remain sterile when stored and will develop a strong odour. Most people find the smell of other people's urine more offensive than their own. Always use fresh urine, no more than 2–3 hours old.

WASHING SODA SPRAY

Use this spray for downy mildew on grapes, melons, peas, pumpkins, zucchini, pansies and other ornamentals. Dissolve 110 g washing soda in 5.5 L cold water. Add 55 g soft soap. Spray at once.

CHAPTER FIVE

PESTS

It's a common Western habit to see anything that isn't useful as a nuisance, or to focus on the harm that other creatures may do without seeing their wider roles. Birds may damage fruit but they also control pests and provide invaluable dung. Wallabies can damage trees but may suppress excess weedy growth. We live in a complex world of interacting creatures, plant and animal; if we reduce that complexity we can cause unexpected changes.

Some pests, however, need to be eradicated, or at least rigorously controlled. Introduced pests such as foxes and rabbits and feral cats can devastate a country where the native inhabitants, plants, soil, streams and animals did not evolve needing to cope with them. But it is possible to live with the rest, as the advice below should show.

ANTS

Ants are valuable predators. They may, however, also transfer sap-suckers from plant to plant (to 'milk' their sweet secretions) and ant nests can kill plants above them.

To deter ants:
• Increase humus levels with plenty of mulch and keep the garden moist, with drip irrigation if possible.

• Move pots regularly to stop ants building nests in and around them.

• Pour hot tea remnants on pot plants and use tea leaf mulch.

• Place a ring of talcum powder around pot plants, in or on paving, or under the washing line; wherever ants are a nuisance.

To eradicate ants:
• Scatter a bait of 1 part borax or derris to 4 parts icing sugar or peanut butter or mince around their nests.

• Spray nests with 1 part kerosene, 1 part liquid detergent and 1 part vegetable oil. Straight kerosene or diesel can also be used, but will not penetrate as far or be as effective.

• Pour a bucket of boiling water down the nest, wait 10 minutes, then spray the ants on the surface with a pyrethrum-based spray.

• Apply tree-banding grease around shrubs or on the base of seedlings.

BIRDS

Birds are the best predators of all to help control pests, and they are also wonderful companions. I happily grow extra fruit and vegetables to share with the birds; it's a small price to pay for the joy of watching them.

To control bird damage:
• Plant native fruit suitable for your area. Birds prefer acid native fruit, which is why they eat unripe non-native fruit. Commercial orchards have found that a barrier of native fruit ripening at the same time as the commercial crop keeps birds away from the valuable crop.

• Provide fresh water near fruit trees. Some birds, especially small birds such as silvereyes, only want moisture, not the fruit itself.

• Use bird netting while the fruit is ripening. These nets can be re-used, and need only be in place for a few weeks of the year.

• Try decoy fruit. Birds are conservative and will finish one crop before starting on another. We keep the birds off our apples by putting out boxes of last year's kiwi fruit just before the apples are ripening. They keep eating the old kiwi fruit until we've picked the apples. We later safeguard our kiwi fruit crop by feeding the birds old, bruised apples.

• Try loud noises, as for flying foxes or fruit bats (see p. 45), scare guns, or radio.

• Hang strings of aluminium foil or inflated bladders from casks of wine or fruit juice in the trees (this has varying success and none with cockatoos).

• Hawk kites can be every effective for short periods, but unless they are moved often, the birds get used to them. They can also scare away chooks and small pest-eating birds.

• Brush bitter substances on the fruit — either commercial preparations or chilli sauce.

This may keep many species of birds away, if they have another good food supply.

• Hang large drawings of eyes on wood or cardboard on the trees. These will scare small birds such as silvereyes.

• Tape birds' alarm calls and replay them sporadically through the day, especially in the early morning.

• Study birds to find out when they do most damage. Often it will be in the early morning; concentrate on bird-scaring tactics then.

CATS

See also Cats, p. 11. To deter cats from hunting birds, tie two warning bells on them, and have dry feed available at all times. Give cats their own dug garden, a good scratching post or two, and interesting plants such as cat thyme, cat grass or catnip. Play with them often and keep them inside at night so they cannot attack roosting birds or sleeping lizards. Make sure all trees and bushes have cat barriers on them to protect birds. The onus is on you to protect surrounding wildlife and to ensure that your cats cannot stray. If they do, it's not the cats' fault, it's yours; cats are born to hunt and roam.

• Cover bare earth and sandpits with bird netting. When cats try to scratch in it and get their paws caught they will learn not to use that particular bit of ground. Wire netting is also effective, but more cumbersome.

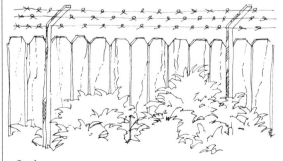

Cat fence

*To get rid of sawfly larvae, shake or prune twigs on which they are clustered,
or use a derris spray on the leaves.*

Most ladybird species are valuable pest predators; here, larvae attack aphids on a hibiscus bud.

Fruit fly can devastate fruit and vegetable crops. Control them with a combination of orchard hygiene and traps, baits, repellents and sprays.

The Mediterranean fruit fly, pictured, and the Queensland fruit fly are the varieties common in Australia.

Cat guard

• Make a barrier around the garden with a hedge of gooseberries or any other thickly growing prickly plant, such as miniature roses.

• Try the dog repellent below, or a barrier of white pepper or mothballs.

• As a last resort, keep cats in — or out — with a cat fence; attach a piece of smooth metal or two or three taut barbed wires to your fence so that it slopes over the fence and cats cannot jump out. (Make sure cats cannot climb onto sheds or branches, however, and get out that way.)

• Make a cat guard with a square of aluminium attached around a tree branch, as shown in the illustration above.

DOGS

Dogs may lift their legs or squat to mark their territory. To keep dogs from marking the garden, hose it often to remove other scents.

Deterrents include:
• A string of mothballs on shrubs or fences.

• A scatter of pepper.

• A repellent spray of 1 part chilli, 1 part ammonia, 1 part horseradish or wormwood, 1 part vinegar and 6 parts water. Let it sit overnight then spray on fences or around

shrubs, not on tender leaves.

• *Coleus caninus*, or dog bane, which smells as though a dog has just lifted its leg there. Some dogs do avoid it; others ignore it. A thick wormwood hedge may also repel dogs.

FLYING FOXES OR FRUIT BATS

The only sure way to keep fruit bats off is to buy specially designed nets to keep them out (ordinary bird netting or old mosquito nets will not work).

Fruit bats usually prefer native fruit to crops. However, if native fruit ripens just before the crop, it may simply attract bats to your garden. They will eat the native fruit and then move into the fruit trees. Grow a wide variety of native fruits when crops are ripening. If using deterrents, remember that deterrents won't work if there is no other source of food for the pest.

Deterrents include:
• Paper bags impregnated with a strong smelling oil such as eucalyptus, lavender or wintergreen, then placed over the fruit. Wintergreen oil, which is the most effective of these repellents, can also be brushed over branches. Urine-impregnated paper bags can also be used.

• Mothballs hung through the branches.

• Loud noises, especially of a high frequency. Thses will work until bats get used to them.

• Radio left on a 'talking' channel (bats will soon get used to this, too).

• Fishing line strung between branches.

• Flashing coloured lights.

GRASSHOPPERS AND LOCUSTS

Locust plagues are a result of white settlement. A swarm of plague locusts can defoliate a garden in a couple of days. Conventional gardening and farming advice is to spray any of the grasshopper/locust pests with a 0.1 Maldison spray. Like most conventional pest control measures, this will kill them but not control them. More will breed up elsewhere and migrate to the garden where you may have killed the predators (especially birds) that would have helped keep them under control.

The best control is long-term, and largely out of suburban gardeners' hands. Leave as much bush as possible, don't drain swamps, do make new ones, avoid pesticides and encourage birds with water, shelter and flowering shrubs.

To control grasshoppers and locusts:
• Increase the area of greenery around the garden, especially of tough-leaved plants such as grevilleas, bitter plants such as wormwood, or poisonous plants such as rhubarb or lobelias (although in a really bad plague grasshoppers will eat all these, too). In several plagues here our gardens surrounded by bush were attacked but not devastated, while others surrounded by bare paddocks were wiped out.

Rows of marigolds, larkspurs, pyrethrum, lobelias, tomatoes or rhubarb are supposed to deter locusts and grasshoppers. I've tried them with no success whatsoever. This was in the drought, however; they may act as a mild deterrent in better conditions.

• Try overhead spraying around the perimeter of a garden; locusts and grasshoppers do not like flying through water. I protected young citrus trees one year by punching holes in the line that fed the drip irrigation system. Each young tree was protected by a fine spurt of water. Microjets with good water pressure should do as well. Avoid perforated hoses; there is a fine balance between deterring grasshoppers and saturating the soil. Turn the system off at dusk.

• Make a grasshopper repellent. Grind 10 chillies, 1 garlic bulb, 1 onion and 1 tablespoon

horseradish. Add 4 cups water. Leave for 24 hours. Strain and spray every couple of days. This is only effective for mild invasions.

• Make small locust traps. Fill old paint tins or wide-mouthed jars with a mixture of 1 part molasses to 9 parts water. Cover with a film of oil to deter bees and mosquitoes. Place as many as possible around the crops.

• Make a large-scale locust trap. Float a piece of yellow plastic in a child's inflatable swimming pool or any other large body of water. Locusts will jump onto the plastic and drown.

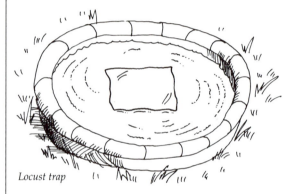
Locust trap

• Let chooks and turkeys loose in the garden. These definitely reduce crop losses. During one mild plague we let chooks loose in our garden, especially in the early morning when the locusts were still lethargic, or at dusk when the locusts were slowing down and the chooks were sated with green feed and unlikely to attack the lettuce.

• Pick them off. My father's anti-grasshopper technique is to get up at dawn, when the pests are stationary, put on a pair of gloves and run his hands over the plants that the grasshoppers prefer. Any he finds, he squashes.

• Use only sprays that break down quickly, such as derris. Spray the leaves that the grasshoppers or locusts will eat.

• Cover plants with tulle. A friend swathed

her entire garden with white tulle; it was remarkably effective for weeks but, as this was the mother of all grasshopper plagues, eventually the 'hoppers ate the tulle. In lesser plagues this would work like a charm.

POSSUMS

There are two choices with possums: put up with them or remove them. The latter will probably mean their deaths; possums are very territorial and will trek for kilometres to return home. Other possums will kill them or let them starve before they let them stay in their area. Remember: a pair of resident possums will keep out strange possums and at least you will know your residents' habits.

To control possums:
• Feed them regularly with sweet thing like apples, or leftover bread or carrot tops. They will be less inclined to go for the rose buds.

• Use deterrents to keep them off new growth: cayenne pepper, chilli sauce, bitter aloes or spray the plants with *fresh* urine (no older than 2–3 hours, as stale urine will burn the foliage).

• Net shrubs when they have a lot of new growth.

• Enclose your eaves with net so they cannot settle in your roof, where suburban possums mostly live. If the possums have to be removed before it is possible to net, try a loud radio, or leave a light on in the roof space during the day. As a last resort hire a mobile disco for half an hour of flashing lights and noise. This gets rid of possums at once; then net the roof space straight away.

RABBITS
To deter rabbits:
• Make a rabbit-proof fence of chicken wire, at least one metre high, to stop them getting into the garden. Bury it 15 cm deep, or leave a 15 cm 'skirt' above ground on the outside of the fence, weighed down by heavy rocks. If wombats start pushing through the fence, make heavy gates on hinges for them.

• Use a low-level electric fence. If the electricity to the fence is turned off, rabbits will however forget about the shock and barge through. Also, for safety reasons, the fence should have only a small amount of electricity passing through it, so that it is easily shorted out by long grass or bracken.

• Tie old aluminium foil or tarpaper around the base of young trees to prevent rabbits ringbarking them. Tie the barriers on with string, which should rot in a year or so and will not ringbark the tree as it gets bigger. An old tin can opened at the side and jammed around the trunk will work, too, but will ringbark the tree if left and seems to encourage fungal and bacterial diseases in the bark.

• Try a ring of old tyres two deep around the trees. This will keep off rabbits and act as mulch. The added warmth as the black tyres absorb and retain heat will help tree growth as well. Remember to take off the tyres while the trees are still small; they can be impossible to cut through and you may be left with an ugly tyre or two around the tree forever.

• Grow crops that might attract rabbits in gardens made from old tyres. The tyre smell will also discourage wombats. Tyre gardens warm up faster and stay warmer in winter and so they are good for early and late crops such as tomatoes and cucumbers.

• Use rabbit deterrents (these will only work if the rabbits are not starving). Try wood ash, chilli sauce or cayenne pepper sprinkled on foliage for a short-term solution (i.e. until it rains or you want to water or the wind blows them off). Spray with bitter aloe spray (available at chemists, or use aloe squeezed from home-grown aloe plants) or quassia spray.

An old-fashioned but effective remedy is kerosene mixed with dripping. Melt 6 parts fat, take off the heat and stir in 1 part kerosene. Do not reheat. Paint on with a tough wide brush. Wear gloves. Apply to tree trunks only, not to soft foliage.

The smell of blood and bone or human urine also makes plants less attractive to rabbits.

• Use rabbit repellents. Paint trunks with white paint; this works and will not wash off.

The following mixture is also effective, but secure fencing is better. Dissolve 3 kg powdered rosin (available at music and ballet supply shops) in 4 L denatured alcohol (not wood or methyl alcohol, which won't dissolve the rosin). Place the alcohol and rosin in an airtight container and shake, then leave for a day or two. Do not apply heat and make sure no water gets into the solution. Paint it round the bark at the tree bases. Don't use on foliage. The repellent won't wash off, although rain may turn it white, and it should work for about a year. Prepare only the amount required, as this mixture doesn't keep.

SLUGS AND SNAILS

Most plants recover well from pest damage and some may even be helped by the extra 'pruning'. Plants that have been badly eaten by snails, however, never fully recover and will always grow more slowly and be more vulnerable to disease and other pest attacks. The reasons for this are still unclear.

The best way to control your slug and snail population is with large numbers of birds. A kookaburra can crack and eat six snails in half an hour. Many lizards eat slugs and snails, as do frogs and toads. Unfortunately, snails are usually at their worst in spring, when seedlings are being planted and lizards are not yet sufficiently awake.

Gardens can be designed to minimise slug and snail damage. Ensure plants are healthy; sappy, nitrogen-fed growth is more likely to attract slug and snail damage. Clean up patches of grass and weeds that offer shelter. I stopped snail damage on the cabbages by moving away the slow compost heap. Mulch can also harbour snails. Speed up its decomposition with a scatter of blood and bone or pelletised hen manure or even a sprinkle of urine.

Deterrents include:

• Irritating barriers of slaked lime, crushed eggshells, diatomite, dry wood ash, finely chopped human hair, sharp grit, and broken shells.

• Salt. This is the most effective barrier but it can be toxic in the garden. Buy 1.25 cm black polythene pipe, cut out the top third, fill it with salt, seal off the ends by tying them with wire, then drape the pipe around the garden as a snail fence. Snails will not cross it and the barrier is easily moved, but be careful that it does not overflow into the garden during rain.

• Watering with wormwood spray or Bordeaux spray. Both will repel slugs and snails, but wormwood spray is preferable. Bordeaux can deposit too much copper in the soil (killing ladybirds and other predators).

Try also:

• Snail fences. Edge the garden with a barrier of thin metal, about 40 cm high, with a downwards-pointing edge angled outwards. Snails will be unable to climb over and will shelter under the ledge so you can easily destroy them.

Make an electric snail fence with fuse wire and a large torch battery and ice cream sticks. (Don't laugh, it works.) The fence should be about 2 mm above the ground.

Make a cheaper fence by surrounding the garden with tin cans with the tops and

Snail fence

bottoms cut out. Press them into the soil so they stand shoulder to shoulder in a long line. A similar fence with sharp edges can be made with cut-off soft drink bottles but the plastic will turn brittle in the sun.

• Copper barriers. Slugs and snails usually won't cross copper. Surround your garden with a band of copper or wrap narrow bands round susceptible plants such as cabbages. The copper can be removed and used again.

• Snail soup. This is the most effective repellent; unfortunately it only works on the type of snail it's made from. Use snails from your own garden. It is also disgusting and should only be made by those with strong stomachs.

First catch the snails, preferably on a wet night. Crush them and throw them into a bucket of water. Put the lid on and leave for a few weeks. Spray the resulting liquid over the seedlings once a week and give the final sludge to your plants; it is high in calcium, nitrogen and phosphorous.

• Baits and traps. Many people do not succeed with snail traps because they have not used the right bait for their area. *Snails are conservative feeders.* They will be attracted to foods similar to the ones they are used to.

Baits include hollowed-out raw potatoes; squeezed grapefruit or orange halves; empty beer cans (leave them in the garden overnight, and they'll fill up with snails or slugs); cans filled with bran or wheatgerm; and/or wilted cabbage leaves smeared with dripping.

No home-made snail bait will be as convenient to use, or as attractive to slugs and snails, as commercial pellets. Home-made bait is, however, cheaper and less toxic. My favourite bait is made from 1 part bran, 1 part derris dust, 2 parts grated raw potato, moistened with a little molasses. The snails eat it, froth up and die, but birds and pets can safely eat the bait or the dying poisoned snails.

Alternatively, place commercial pellets in old margarine containers. Leave the lids on but cut a small door out of the sides so the slugs and snails can get at the bait. This way birds and pets cannot eat the bait, and as it is not in contact with the soil, it will not kill earthworms and other soil life either.

• A permanent trap. Fill an ice cream container with water. Scatter a thick layer of bran onto the surface. Leave the trap almost submerged in the garden. The snails will crawl up, in and drown (if they like bran).

• Ducks and hens. Only well-trained ducks can be left in the garden all day to hunt snails. Other ducks will eat the garden as well as the snails. Buy them young or fully trained and choose active ducks like Khaki Campbells or Indian Runners.

Give ducks plenty of green feed but no protein all day, then let them into the garden for an hour or so in the late afternoon, so that they go for the snails and pests. Only give them concentrates after a hard day's snail clearing.

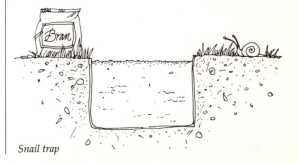
Snail trap

Let hens into the vegetable garden for the last hour before they perch. By then they should have had enough green stuff and will eat the slugs and snails without tearing up the garden. This only works with free range hens; confined chooks, unless they have been given a lot of greens, will tear into the vegetables without a thought for the snails.

WALLABIES

Of all the animals in our garden, the wallabies do most damage, pulling down, and usually breaking, fruit tree branches to get to the young shoots. Train your trees tall so that the lower banches are out of wallaby reach.

We try to fence the wallabies out but there is always one clever one who slips between the wires or wriggles through a new wombat hole. (We also put in wombat gates.) Most rabbit repellents (see p. 48) also work with wallabies. With both wallabies and rabbits, fencing is the only long-term solution.

After many years of anti-wallaby efforts, I have decided that the best answer lies in netting susceptible trees and pruning off low branches, then taking the nets off when the branches are out of wallaby reach. We also grow plants that wallabies dislike: lavender, rosemary, prickly grevilleas, daffodils, wormwood, jonquils, poppies, lilies and others.

Deterrents include:

• Firewater spray or stale wine. This stops wallabies nibbling until rain washes off the taste. (Use sparingly on the soil because it can burn plants.) Mix white pepper, dried or chopped fresh chillies and chopped fresh horseradish (if available). Pour hot vinegar and water over the lot, then leave the mixture to stand for a week. Strain well and spray.

• Wire tree guards.

• Human hair in old pantyhose.

• See also Rabbits, p. 48, for kerosene and dripping deterrent. The smell of blood and bone or hen manure keeps off wallabies.

CHAPTER SIX

FRUIT BUSHES AND TREES

MAJOR PESTS AND DISEASES

CODLING MOTH

Control of codling moth is not easy by any method, organic or otherwise, but it is possible without high residue pesticides. This requires several years' work and constant vigilance after that. This method should, however, also reduce other pests, such as light brown apple moth and scale, as natural predators build up.

The battle against codling moths requires an understanding of their life cycle. Codling moths are an introduced pest. They originated in Europe and gained their common name from the wild codling tree from which modern varieties of apples are derived. They have no native food sources, only orchard ones: apples, and to a lesser extent pears, hawthorn fruit, walnuts, quinces, peaches, nectarines and plums as well as eggplant, occasionally. Even with these alternative foods nearby, codling moths will probably stick to apple trees. If they are proving hard to eradicate, however, check these alternate homes.

Codling moths lay their eggs on or near the fruit when the temperature is 15°C or more. The eggs look like tiny flat circular scales. They hatch in one or two weeks, depending on temperature, and the young caterpillar enters the fruit, usually from the top or bottom, and chews its way down into it.

This is the part of the caterpillar's life that causes the damage and is the hardest to control. The caterpillar may eat the seeds, causing the fruit to drop, or the apple may rot or, if the infection was late, the caterpillar may still be there when the fruit is consumed.

When feeding is completed (after three to five weeks), the caterpillars commonly shelter either on the butts of trees or in wooden objects near trees (old ladders and fruit boxes and corners of sheds). There the caterpillars spin cocoons. The moths usually emerge in spring, though there can be several hatchings a year. Caterpillars in cocoons can also remain dormant for up to two years. Adult moths shelter in the foliage during the day and become active at dusk and just before dawn.

The peak time of adult activity is October to December, with another hatching in December to January. There can be three cycles (hatchings) of codling moth a season, which makes control of long-maturing apples such as Granny Smith particularly difficult.

In a CSIRO experiment in Victoria, begun in 1975, 36 apple trees were placed in wire cages which moths could neither escape from nor enter. In spite of exhaustive searches and two sprayings of ryania, the pest was not wiped out in the enclosures until 1977.

Once codling moth has been eradicated, there is a good chance of keeping it away. Female codling moths rarely travel more than 50 metres and males no more than 200 metres. If codling moth can be eliminated in the area, and you can prevent reinfestation, chances of a large-scale reinfestation are slight.

Control of the codling moth inside the apple by organic means is difficult; by definition, organic remedies usually break down before control can be achieved. Therefore, rely on rigorous orchard hygiene and on controlling the moths and caterpillars *before* they get to the apples.

The individual control measures below will eliminate *some* codling moth. Combined, they are more effective and together with the orchard hygiene techniques, also below, should eliminate most of the pest.

ORCHARD HYGIENE

As soon as apples form, they must be checked every ten days for holes in tops and bottoms. Caterpillars feed for three to five weeks in apples (sometimes in more than one apple) before they pupate. As they feed, more detritus gets pushed out of the hole: check for this as a symptom. All infected apples must be removed and burnt, or fed to animals, but not buried or composted. Let animals (chooks, sheep, pigs, wombats) graze under the trees. Any fruit that falls is likely to be infected (damage to the seeds causes the apples to fall).

Remove all old boxes and ladders from the orchard and do not bring in second-hand ones. Check corners of sheds regularly for cocoons. Check flowering and crab apples, quinces and any apples in storage. (Picked apples may also be infected or signs of damage may yet emerge.)

Remember: any moth that escapes means a thousand more at the end of the season.

CATERPILLAR CONTROL

1. When caterpillars have finished feeding they travel down the branches and trunk looking for a place to pupate, unless the fruit they are in has already fallen. You can trap caterpillars by scraping the loose bark from the trunk and main branches of the trees. Then fix to the trunk either a corrugated cardboard band or a pile of old wool, soaked in liquid derris or old sump oil. Inspect every week and get rid of trapped pupae. The most important times for trapping are winter and spring but for effective control inspect the bands all year.

2. Grease-band trunks and large branches to prevent larvae finding places to cocoon. Bands should be in place from the first moth sighting until midwinter.

3. Run animals such as hens under trees and avoid sprays that may kill other predators. A wide range of birds feeds on caterpillars, as do spiders, ants, many types of wasps, hoverflies and their larvae; the combined effect of these can be dramatic.

MOTH CONTROL

Lure pots. Lure pots are an ineffective method of control in themselves as not all moths will find them. They will, however, indicate when to spray and the extent of the codling moth infestation.

To make a lure pot, fill a glass jar with 1 part port to 7 parts water, or 1 part molasses to 10 parts water. Top up with a little oil to deter mosquitoes and stop moths escaping. Hang them at about shoulder height in the trees in the warmest part of the orchard, where codling moths are likely to be active first. Renew the contents every week, or after every large rainstorm, and inspect for drowned corpses every morning.

Other moths may also be attracted to the bait. Note: codling moths are about 20 mm from wing to wing, greyish-brown, with a circular, slightly shiny, dark area near each wing tip.

Pheromone traps. These commercially available traps will only trap the male codling moth (which thinks it is being lured to a female in a receptive state). One male codling moth can cover a lot of territory; codling moths are not monogamous, unfortunately. Rigorous trap use, following the manufacturer's directions, can limit infestation to a rate of about 5%; in other words, five out of every hundred fruit will be affected. This is satisfactory as long as you ensure that none of the moths in the infected fruit hatch in storage and infect the rest of the crop. (Many organic apples appear to be infected with codling moth after they have left the grower, when they are in storage areas with poor hygiene.)

Pheromone traps are probably more useful for the large-scale grower than for backyard use; combined with other control measures, they can be very useful indeed.

Sprays. For individual spray recipes, refer to Chapter Four, Organic Remedies (or see index).

Use a derris spray on and underneath leaf tips as soon as the first moth sighting is made. This will kill moths hiding in the foliage, and may kill some of the caterpillars in the short time before they disappear into the apples. After the initial spray, spray in crevices and under the leaves, as that is where the moths will be hiding, not on top of the leaves. Do not spray derris more than once a fortnight.

If the temperature is below 24°C, use a light oil spray. This will destroy eggs, but will also damage foliage in hotter weather. Spray above and below the leaves every ten days. At the same time, spray Dipel directly onto the apples. Continue this weekly until no more moths are found trapped by the lures. It will have only a limited effect, but will add to the general destruction and is less harmful than derris, which kills other inhabitants of the orchard.

The plant-derived insecticide ryania is reasonably species-specific, though it will kill beetles and other caterpillars. It kills the codling moth caterpillars after they have burrowed into the apple. Unfortunately, ryania is far less effective in hotter, harsher Australia than in the northern hemisphere.

Companion planting. There are two companion plants that aid codling moth control: nasturtiums and parsnips, gone to seed. Both rely on attracting predators that eat the moths and caterpillars. I know of no nasturtium trials. Leaving parsnips to flower under the trees and through the orchards has been tried in several places (including my own small plot of apples) and is an extremely successful repellent. Let the parsnips naturalise. They are hard to grow at first: their seed only lasts a year at most and much commercial seed is no longer viable. Once the first crop sets seed and and the seed blows around the orchard, parsnips spring up all over the place. A few seasons of this and they should be flowering most of the year. Slash them occasionally as you would grass and let more flower heads spring up.

FRUIT FLY

There is no easy, single way to control fruit fly organically. Organic fruit fly control requires a combination of fruit fly lures, baits or traps and orchard hygiene methods (which also help protect trees' general health and vigour).

Two sorts of fruit fly are common in Australia: the Queensland fruit fly and the Mediterranean fruit fly. Both have similar life cycles and under law must be controlled. I've never used conventional fruit fly controls (apart from two trial periods when comparing the effectiveness of various control measures) and I've been selling fruit that is susceptible to fruit fly — apricots, peaches, citrus, apples — for twenty years. In the long term, using fruit fly sprays may make trees more pest-prone by killing off other natural pest predators.

ORCHARD HYGIENE

This is essential. No fruit fly control measure, organic or otherwise, will work if there are thousands of fruit fly breeding around the garden.

1. Pick up fallen fruit. This must be done within a day of its falling. Even a couple of days' neglect can cause a pest explosion. Infected fruit tends to fall from the tree before it is ripe, as the larvae burrow to the centre of the fruit, damaging the seeds in the core and causing it to fall. Most fruit fly breed on the ground, not on the tree.

Pick up every apricot, every windfall apple, every squashy overripe tomato. Feed the fallen fruit to animals, cover it with water for three weeks in a bucket or bin (with a lid on or a thin layer of oil to stop mosquitoes breeding) or place it in a sealed garbage bag in the sun until the fruit inside decomposes.

The easiest way to keep fallen fruit off the ground is to run animals such as geese and wombats under the trees. Let chooks out under the trees for an hour every morning. Pay someone to pick fruit off the ground. Make the fallen fruit into chutney or jam once the bad bits are removed.

Fruit fly die off in cold winters. A combination of cold winters and garden and orchard hygiene may prevent them from building up to problem proportions until summer crops are harvested.

2. Avoid early- and late-ripening crops. These include loquats in bad fruit fly areas. Their spring fruit may attract the fly to later crops. Be careful of late summer fruits such as quinces, figs and medlars, which can host fruit fly and provide a bridge period for the fruit fly to breed in, ready to infect winter crops such as citrus. A fruit fly-free gap of a couple of months may be enough to save later crops from infection.

3. Separate ripening fruit crops. We 'time' our orchards. Most fruit fly travel up our valley. The earliest ripening fruit, early apricots, are nearest the road. By the time fruit fly get here, the apricots have finished. The next orchard of ripe stone fruit is some distance away, across a creek and a large patch of hill and bush. By the time fruit fly find it, that orchard too is finished. (If we allowed the fruit to stay on the ground, breeding fruit fly, this would fail; fruit fly can fly 5 kilometres, and our methods could not cope with a large influx of them.)

Never plant trees that will fruit just when a neighbouring crop is finishing. Let them fruit all together or allow a month between crops. Plant early varieties; early apricots or peaches may fruit before the fruit fly begin to build up.

4. Check your compost. Slow compost is a perfect breeding ground for fruit fly, even if it does not contain fruit. See pp. 15–17 for more details on compost management.

5. Check your neighbourhood. Stone fruit often ripens during the Christmas break, when neighbours are away on holidays and fruit fly numbers are building up under their peach trees. Offer to pick up their fruit (it will be suitable for jam). Offer them the pickings of your trees when you go away as a return favour. As a last resort, report neighbours who do not control fruit fly.

6. Control. No matter how good the prevention, fruit fly numbers will gradually build up over summer; they probably fly in from somewhere else.

COMBINE GARDEN HYGIENE METHODS WITH:

Baits. Fruit fly fly for about a week before they mate and lay eggs. If they are killed in this time, the breeding cycle is broken. Baits and traps are very effective and provide the continuous control needed. Their main disadvantage is that they may actually attract fruit fly to the area.

DAK pots, commercially available traps, are only useful to indicate if fruit fly are present. DAK pots attract only male Queensland fruit fly, whereas it is the females that lay eggs. The Mediterranean fruit fly is the main species active in Western Australia.

Beer bait. Simplest of all, open bottles or cans of beer around the garden. Beer is sweet, wet and yeasty, all the things that fruit fly like. Add a little detergent to each beer container to make it stickier. As the fruit fly try to feed they are caught in the wet, sticky surface. This may keep fruit fly down to reasonable numbers, as long as they are not breeding nearby.

Cheat's five-minute ginger beer. For every litre of water add ½ cup sugar (for human consumption, reduce the sugar), 1 sliced lemon and ½ teaspoon powdered or root ginger. Boil for 5 minutes. When tepid, add a pinch of dried yeast. Leave overnight then bottle. It should be ready the same day but is usually best after three days. It will catch fruit flies for at least a fortnight, sometimes a month. For human consumption, this ginger beer lasts between one and two weeks.

Pesticides. In commercial orchards where labour is scarce, it may be necessary to use a longer-lasting pesticide. A commercial splash-on bait is available which combines a protein hydrolysate bait with Maldison. This is not organic but as the bait can be splashed onto the tree trunks, rather than sprayed through the tree, the effect on you and the surroundings is limited. I recommend this if neighbours are not controlling their fruit fly.

A home-made organic bait can be made with 50 g sugar in 1 L water. Add 7 ml concentrated pyrethrum (see p. 38). Splash on the trees; do not spray, as the result will be too diluted to be effective. Apply from two weeks before and up to one week after the known fruit fly dates in your district, or until two weeks after the last fruit has been harvested, whichever is the later date. Apply at least every week as pyrethrum breaks down on contact with light. This bait is not as effective or long-lasting as the Maldison bait.

Repellent. This keeps away small numbers of fruit fly, as well as possums, dogs and cats. The smell is overpowering and it is not organic (so avoid skin contact).

Mix 1 L kerosene, 1 L creosote and a packet of mothballs. Place it in your orchard in tins about 10 metres apart, hung from fruit trees. In the vegetable garden, place the tins at about 4 metre intervals. Mothballs hung from trees also have a limited repellent value.

Traps. Two years ago I left two boxes of various fruit fly baits in the kitchen. I had a nice fruit fly-infected carton of peaches ready to test the baits with. At the same time I was mixing up a batch of ginger beer. The fruit fly ignored the baits (including commercial ones) and dived into the ginger beer, so I began experimenting with ginger beer in fruit fly traps.

Cover the ginger beer bottles with old mosquito netting or flyscreen wire so bees and wasps do not become inebriated. Now hang the bottles in the fruit trees or tie them to a stake among the tomatoes. (Alternatively, the top of a soft-drink bottle can be inverted in a bucket and filled with ginger beer, as illustrated below.) Three bottles are needed for a large tree. (Don't put too many out until you know fruit fly are present or they may be attracted by the bottles.) Add a little oil to the top of the bottle as in some areas fruit fly seem to be able to drink, then fly away.

A bait of 9 parts molasses and 1 part water with a pinch of yeast can be used, or a couple of banana peels in water with a pinch of yeast, bran, sugar and hot water. 1 part human urine to 10 parts water, with an orange rind and a pinch of yeast per bottle, will also work.

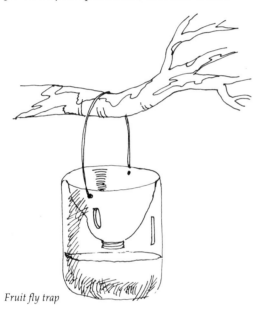

Fruit fly trap

Wormwood and sour milk spray (see p. 40 and add 1 part sour milk to 1 part wormwood mixture). I have experimented with this for the last two years; it is still too early to say how effective it is, but so far the results seem good. Spray every two weeks during the season and after rain or overhead watering.

FERMENT FLIES

Tiny flies that hover around the fruit bowl are probably harmless ferment flies. These will not attack healthy fruit on the plant and are not to be confused with fruit fly.

LICHEN

Lichen is a symbiotic association of a fungi and an algae. Lichens can be green to grey, scaly or bushy, soft, hard or stringy; they are in fact not pests but are good for trees because they harbour predators. Lichened fruit trees are less susceptible to pests and diseases than those without lichen.

If you are determined to rid your trees of lichens despite their good qualities, scrub the lichens off or spray Bordeaux in winter, making sure in the case of evergreens to avoid foliage and flowers. Paint Bordeaux on thickly if possible; it will kill the lichen, which will gradually flake off. For a faster result, take up the scrubbing brush again. Be warned: both the Bordeaux and the lack of lichen will reduce the number of predators that may control pests next season.

ROOT ROTS

Root rots are usually indicated by wilting foliage, especially in wet weather, or by gradual or sudden dying back of the tree. Root rots can affect most plants. *Phytophthora cinnamomi* is cinnamon fungus which affects a wide range of plants, from carnations to trees. Large roots are dark and brittle, small roots are absent. With armillaria root rot a white fungal sheath grows over the roots and small yellow toadstools may appear above ground. Trees with root rots are usually shaky when pushed.

PREVENTION

The best prevention for phytophthora is not to bring it in in the first place via muddy boots, infected water, bulldozers and nursery stock.

• For all root rot prevention, maintain high levels of organic matter in the soil. Mulch is essential; make a mulch with one third lucerne, one third wattle tree bark and one third other material — comfrey leaves are excellent, as are nettles.

• Avoid digging in undecomposed organic matter such as manure or green manure. Leave it on top of the soil, roughly slashed. Compost of any sort, especially compost made from the mulch ingredients above, is excellent and inhibits root rots. Add dolomite to raise the pH level and use blood and bone or hen manure as high-phosphorous fertilisers to keep plants growing strongly.

• Make sure drainage is good. Use no-dig methods around trees to avoid injuring roots; mulch and mow instead of digging. If drainage cannot be improved, grow trees in a sloping mound on top of the ground instead of digging them in.

• Avoid harsh artificial fertilisers and high-nitrogen fertilisers. Encourage the soil microflora, imitating rainforest conditions as far as possible: high levels of undisturbed organic matter, moist soil with no sudden sodden bursts from overhead irrigation.

Once trees have been infected with root rots, try cutting them back as an emergency measure so the damaged roots have less foliage to support. Give the trees a foliar spray once a week until the roots reestablish: seaweed spray is excellent, or cover some good compost with water and spray when it is weak tea colour.

With luck, this will keep the tree growing while you work on the major problems. Improve drainage and soil pH, and mulch with good compost or lucerne hay or wilted comfrey until the natural soil microorganisms can get the rots under control and the roots can reestablish themselves.

If trees must be dug out, remove *all* the roots and burn them. Dig well beyond the drip line to ensure they are all gone. Leave the hole open to the air for at least six months. A large bonfire on the site before replanting will ensure all infected debris is removed. If only one tree is infected, it may be worthwhile digging it out at once before infection spreads, especially if it is up the slope from other trees, where water will carry the infection down.

Armillaria root rot can be prevented by making sure all old tree roots (orchard trees, wattles, etc.) are removed before replanting. If the trees do become infected, expose the roots (for about 60 cm around the trunk) to sunlight. Cut away dead roots. Fill the hole with fresh soil when the infection seems to be clear. Do not replace soil with mulch or compost, or water may pool in the hole. Use a slightly richer feeding regime than usual until the tree picks up vigour.

WOOD ROTS

Wood rots can affect most trees. Thin, frilly fungi or dark, dead wood are the main symptoms.

CONTROL

Most wood-rotting fungi only attack dead wood, injured branches or unhealthy trees. Waterlogged or starved trees are particularly susceptible. Take care pruning, make sure drainage is good and keep trees growing steadily. Cut out all affected wood down to healthy tissue. Keep the plant growing strongly so that healthy wood closes over the wound as soon as possible.

PROBLEMS

For individual spray recipes, refer to Chapter Four, Organic Remedies (or see index).

ALMOND

See also Peach, pp. 72–73.

FAILURE TO FRUIT
Solution: Almonds need two cross-pollinating trees, although single trees will occasionally bear fruit. Even so-called cross-pollinators may fail to flower at the same time if they are in slightly different conditions. Multigraft trees are a reliable way to ensure good pollination.

APPLE

APPLE DIMPLING BUG
Symptoms: Dimples in apples. These cause purely cosmetic damage and do not harm the fruit. Do not confuse these with the corky dimples of bitter pit.
Solution: Rely on bird and wasp predators or try bug juice.

BITTER PIT
Symptoms: Sunken circular areas in the skin of the apple and soft granular flesh underneath which breaks down quickly in storage.
Solution: Bitter pit occurs when apples do not take up enough calcium as they mature. It is a long-term problem which can be precipitated by heavy pruning, too much nitrogen or a very dry season.

Add dolomite to the soil: this may take up to two seasons to work. Add wood ash and seaweed mulch if handy. Try a foliar spray from compost or comfrey every second morning for two weeks. A calcium spray may not be organic but it is a useful short term solution.

BRYOBIA AND EUROPEAN MITES
Symptoms: Tiny, reddish, granular patches on stems, branches and trunk.
Solution: Use an oil spray when trees are dormant (not fruiting). See control measures for Red spider mites, p. 59.

CANKER
Symptoms: Blackish bark, possibly splitting, and dead wood.
Solution: Canker results from spores entering a pruning wound or other injury. A winter Bordeaux spray will kill canker spores on the tree; spray before pruning. Paint large wounds with Bordeaux paste. Prune in summer.

CODLING MOTH
See Codling moth, pp. 51–53.

COLLAR AND OTHER WOOD ROTS
Solution: Cut away as much affected wood as possible and paint with Bordeaux paste. Expose affected roots to the air where possible. Feed trees with compost or good mulch, especially rotten lucerne or comfrey leaves. Well-fed trees are more resistant to collar rot, as long as decomposing organic matter is kept away from the tree trunk.

FAILURE TO FRUIT, DROPPED FRUIT
Don't overprune; apples fruit on older spurs and heavy pruning can lead to excess foliage on top and less blossom. There may have been insufficient chilling during a warm winter, fluctuating moisture levels or poor pollination (if this is the cause, there may be few seeds in the apples). Codling moth (see pp. 51–53) can also lead to dropped fruit as the seeds are destroyed by the caterpillar.

FRUIT TREE WEEVIL
Symptoms: Wilted branches, sudden or gradual dieback of the tree.

Solution: Remove any branches that overhang very close to the soil. The larvae pupate in the soil and the adults must climb up the branches of the tree to breed. Place grease bands or glue bands on all branches and trunks to break the breeding cycle.

LEAF SPOT

Symptoms: This may cause premature leaf drop.

Solution: Spray with Bordeaux in winter: once for mild cases, or twice for bad cases, at leaf fall and just before bud burst. A spray of 2% urea solution (commercially available) just before leaf fall will help the leaves decompose quickly over winter and stop reinfection next season. This is not strictly organic but it is still good husbandry.

LIGHT BROWN APPLE MOTH

Solution: This native moth has plenty of predators. Encourage birds, spiders, wasps, etc. Remove vegetation such as weeds around the trees to destroy wintering sites; try close grazing by hens or sheep when the trees are dormant. Pheromone traps may be available. See Codling moth, pp. 51–53.

ORIENTAL FRUIT MOTH

Symptoms: Shoots shrivel; larvae may tunnel into the fruit. Stone fruit, pears and quinces can also be affected.

Solution: See Codling moth, pp. 51–53, for preventive techniques. Rely on wasp predators where possible. Cut off affected twigs, use cardboard or hessian bands around the tree from December onwards, inspecting for sheltering insects every two days. Remove and destroy infected fruit at least twice a week. Scrape loose bark off and keep rubbish away from the tree.

POWDERY MILDEW

Symptoms: Leaves and buds are covered with a greyish powder. It is particularly prevalent on Jonathon apples.

Solution: In winter, prune out affected withered shoots and spray with Bordeaux, baking soda spray, Condy's crystals or urine spray. Add extra potash to the soil.

RED SPIDER MITES

Symptoms: Sand-blasted appearance on foliage, usually worse near the bottom of the tree.

Solution: See Roses, p. 123. Check that the mites are still present before acting, because the damage they have done to the foliage will not disappear when the pest is controlled. Control weeds: mulch over them or slash. Use overhead watering in hot, dry times (red spider mites dislike wetness). For commercial orchards it may be worthwhile to purchase predator mites (*Typhlodromus occidentalis*). They are only useful for large areas as they need a large supply of mites to survive.

Try tansy antifeedant spray first, then milk spray, or coriander or anise spray. Oil sprays are effective but should not be used in temperatures above 24°C or within a week of using Bordeaux. Onion, garlic and marigold sprays are effective but will kill predators as well. Use derris as a last resort.

SCAB

Symptoms: Fruit becomes deformed with dark brown, corky patches.

Solution: Spray with Bordeaux when dormant or with full-strength urine. Spray again at bud swell if the problem is severe. A mixture of 1 part urine to 9 parts water can be sprayed in the early morning when the tree is in leaf to stop the problem spreading. Add extra potash to the soil. Feed trees with compost or good mulch, especially rotten lucerne or comfrey leaves. Well-fed trees are more resistant to scab.

THRIPS

Symptoms: Distorted leaves or flowers; premature petal drop; small black droppings.

Solution: Thrips are a problem of 'desert'

orchards where there is nothing but trees, or trees and lucerne or another single-species ground cover. Thrips breed in low-level ground covers (usually weeds) and migrate upwards when the weeds die off in early spring. Flowering ground covers prevent thrips migrating and reaching problem numbers.

Rain or hot dry weather will reduce thrip numbers. Wasps, lacewings, and ladybirds will clear the problem naturally. Try strong jets of water, and frequent overhead spraying.

Some thrips are useful predators of mites and aphids, so don't automatically destroy them.

WOOLLY APHIDS

Symptoms: Sticky, white, woolly ovals on leaves.

Solution: Wait for predators; dab with metholated spirits; squeeze by hand; try a diluted clay spray, or coriander or anise sprays. As a last resort try derris, rhubarb leaf, garlic and elder sprays. These will control but not eradicate the problem. Don't prune too zealously, as this may attract aphids.

APRICOT

APRICOT FRECKLE

Symptoms: This starts as scabby patches on the fruit. They may join together and crack open the fruit.

Solution: See Brown rot, below.

BACTERIAL GUMMOSIS

Symptoms: Pale splotches on the leaves and gum oozing from trunk and branches.

Solution: Prune as little as possible; dip secateurs in vinegar between trees; spray with Bordeaux in winter.

BROWN ROT

Symptoms: Fruit is covered with a brown rot which sometimes has grey spores. Brown rot may also kill blossom (especially in wet

years or hot humid springs), lead to poor fruit set and dieback of twigs.

Solution: Spray trees with Bordeaux in winter. In bad cases spray both at leaf fall and bud swell. Prune off any dead wood when the tree is dormant; remove any twigs that may have died from brown rot and any dried fruit 'mummies'.

In bad years, thin out the fruit so that none is touching. If brown rot starts, pick out affected fruit at once so the spores do not spread. Spray with chamomile tea or chive tea every two days, or garlic spray once a week, until all fruit is picked. Regular spraying with seaweed spray may make the fruit more resistant to brown rot.

DEAD ARM DISEASE

Symptoms: Dieback in branches.

Solution: Dead arm starts from pruning or picking wounds. Prune in summer when wounds can heal quickly; never prune in wet weather or with secateurs that may be infected from another tree. Sterilise them or dip them in vinegar.

FAILURE TO FRUIT

Tree may be too young; there may have been insufficient chilling; late frosts might kill blossom; birds such as silvereyes, bower birds and parrots may eat small fruit or blossom. Heavy pruning may promote foliage at the expense of fruit; there is no need to prune apricots. See Brown rot, above. Thrips may also cause premature petal fall.

FROST DAMAGE

Solution: Cover ground with a thick mulch around the trees before the soil heats up. This will help delay flowering until frosts are over. Large, unthinned trees are less susceptible to frost damage. See also Frost, pp. 21–23.

FRUIT FLY

Symptoms: Brown patches on fruit with maggots inside. See Fruit fly, pp. 53–56.

Foliar sprays and mulch may have saved this orange tree from root rot damage.

Many pot plant pests can be easily removed by hand or with a toothbrush and white oil.

Grow fruit trees close together, with an understorey of native shrubs,
to give them greater resistance to bird and pest damage.

LIGHT BROWN APPLE MOTH
See Apple, p. 59.

POOR FRUIT SET
This may be due to an unusually warm winter with not enough 'freeze hours'; if so, explore other varieties which need less cold. Severe late frosts, waterlogging, fluctuating moisture levels, lack of bees or damage to blossom by birds such as silvereyes may also be causes.

SHOT HOLE
Symptoms: Leaves develop small, brown-ringed holes; fruit is covered with small red blotches.
Solution: See Brown rot, p. 60.

VERTICULUM FUNGUS OR BLACK HEART
Solution: Do not grow apricots near tomatoes, capsicum or potatoes, as spores can be transferred. If in doubt about the soil where you are planting apricots, cover it for three weeks with clear plastic before planting. Try thick companion planting with garlic.

AVOCADO

ANTHRACNOSE FUNGUS
Symptoms: Dark blotches on the fruit.
Solution: Spray with Bordeaux; prune out any dead wood. Use a preventive seaweed spray.

APHIDS
Symptoms: Wilted or malformed leaves. Aphids produce honeydew that causes sooty mould. They also transfer virus diseases.
Solution: Several biological controls are commercially available. These are invaluable for large-scale control, but will only survive as long as there are aphids to feed on. Control those weeds which act as hosts and add mulch. Use grease bands on the trunks of trees to discourage ants. Marigolds, wormwood and nasturtiums planted beneath trees are said to deter aphids, but most avocados are too high for this to be effective.

In most cases, predators will be sufficient control; wait at least three weeks if possible for population build-up of ladybirds and their larvae, lacewings, hoverflies, birds, wasps, etc. Try spraying with dilute Vegemite to encourage lacewings and hoverflies. Try strong jets of water under and on top of the leaves; a dilute clay or pikelet spray, nettle or wormwood spray or seaweed and nettle spray should be effective. As a last resort, use garlic, lantana, onion or pyrethrum sprays. In bad cases, try a reflective aluminium foil mulch under the trees to deter the aphids.

CRATERED SKIN
Solution: This is caused by the fruit spotting bug. Unfortunately, by the time the damage is visible, it is too late to spray; the damage is done and the pests have probably been controlled naturally. See pp. 6–7, Attracting predators.

FAILURE TO FRUIT
Solution: Seedling avocados may may take up to fifteen years to fruit, or may never fruit (although this is rare). Check that you have the correct pollinators; grow windbreaks if wind is strong at flowering; spray with seaweed spray to increase resistance to frost. Fruit may not set in unseasonally cold weather, even without frost. Ensure there are bees present, as with bees the tree may set fruit even without a pollinator. Most avocado blossom does not set so don't panic if most of it falls off; there will probably still be plenty of fruit.

FAILURE TO RIPEN
Avocados usually ripen after being picked, and will not ripen on the tree unless the fruit have been damaged or the tree is at least 18 months to 2 years old. Fruit that are ready to pick are shiny and rounded, with fat or yellowing stalks. All avocados — no matter how immature — will ripen at some stage, but ripe ones will become soft in one to two weeks.

FRUIT BLEMISHES

Solution: Fruit can be marked by hail, sunburn or rubbing against other fruit or branches. Try tall shelter belts between the trees; bananas, non-encroaching bamboo, sugar cane, trellised kiwi fruit or passionfruit.

FRUIT FLY

See Fruit fly, pp. 53–56.

LEAF LOSS

Solution: Some avocados lose their leaves at flowering. Ensure the soil is moist and wait for new leaves to grow. Check for root rots; if the tree wobbles, there is a problem. If the tree has root rot, the leaves may disappear from the top first, or the whole lot may wilt.

Young trees may need temporary shelter against sunburn. If the leaves are yellowing or brown at the edges, try hessian shelters, windbreaks of bananas, pergolas of passionfruit, etc.

PHYTOPHTHORA AND OTHER ROOT ROTS

Symptoms: Trees may yellow or die back quickly, starting at the top.
Solution: A good organic regime should minimise losses from root rot. Keep trees moist, never waterlogged, never dry. See Root rots, pp. 56–57.

SCALE

Symptoms: A massed covering of small scales; wilted new growth; red areas on fruit; sooty mould (stimulated by the excreted honeydew).
Solution: See Scale, pp. 115–16.

STEM END ROT

Symptoms: A blackish, grey-green rot starting at the stem end and progressing up the fruit.
Solution: Carefully clip the fruit from the branch, leaving a short·stalk. Do not pull or twist or the join between stem and fruit may be damaged.

SUN BLOTCH VIRUS

Symptoms: Yellow or red streaks on fruit, bark and leaves.
Solution: There is no cure. Dig out affected plants at once and burn. Buy from reputable nurseries only.

THRIPS

Symptoms: Distorted leaves and flowers; small, black, visible droppings; premature petal fall.
Solution: See Apple, pp. 59–60.

BANANA

BANANA WEEVIL BORER

Solution: This can be prevented by making sure the new suckers are free from grubs. Keep the base of the banana clear of debris and weeds.

FRUIT LOSS DUE TO BIRDS AND FLYING FOXES

Solution: Tear a banana leaf down the centre and wrap it round the fruit. The fruit will ripen just as well when covered. Otherwise, harvest bananas before they are yellow and keep them under cover to ripen slowly. Ripening can be speeded up by wrapping them in a plastic bag with a piece of citrus or an apple. See also Birds, p. 44 and Flying foxes, p. 45.

FAILURE TO FRUIT

This may be due to cool conditions, or allowing too many suckers to develop after the initial bunch is produced. Feed bananas well with compost and old hen manure and give plenty of water while fruiting.

BLUEBERRY

BIRDS

Solution: Enclose the berries in a protective mesh of old pantyhose stretched out on loops of wire or use a bird net. See Birds, p. 44.

CATERPILLARS
(E.G. LIGHT BROWN APPLE MOTH)
See Apple, p. 59.

GREY MOULD AND LEAF SPOT
Solution: Spray with Bordeaux when the bushes are dormant. Keep bushes well mulched. Spray bushes with chamomile and casuarina spray, or chamomile spray every few days at any time of the year when symptoms appear. Cut off all affected fruit and foliage.

SPLIT FRUIT
Solution: Avoid overhead watering; keep blueberries well mulched. Pick regularly and avoid soluble nitrogen fertilisers.

CHERRY

BROWN ROT
Symptoms: Dark, soft patches on fruit.
Solution: See Apricot, p. 60.

CANKER
Symptoms: Dark, splitting bark, dead wood below, possibly exuding gum.
Solution: Spray with Bordeaux when the tree is dormant, preferably just before or after pruning. Canker usually starts from pruning wounds and can lead to the death of a limb. Minimise pruning; little should be necessary after the second year except to limit tree height.

FRUIT TREE ROOT WEEVIL
Symptoms: The larvae of this weevil chew large furrows out of fruit tree roots. The tree may be weakened or show signs of dieback. The adults eat leaves and stems and lay eggs in folded leaves.
Solution: To prevent the adult weevils getting to the top of the tree to feed and lay, band the tree with raw wool or rags, impregnated with a mixture of old sump oil and edible oil.

PEAR AND CHERRY SLUG
Symptoms: Slug-like sawfly larvae skeletonise the leaves and may eventually defoliate the tree.
Solution: See Sawflies, p. 13, p. 127. Encourage bird and wasp predators. Try suffocators such as dehydrated flour browned in the oven, talcum powder, vacuum cleaner contents or dry wood ash dusted over the leaves, but beware of making the soil too alkaline. Use derris spray or pyrethrum spray. Although pear and cherry slugs are not caterpillars, Dipel has been known to be effective on them. Avoid hawthorn hedges nearby as they can be a source of infection. Vigorous cherry trees can tolerate some damage.

SPLIT FRUIT
Solution: Avoid overhead watering and fluctuations in moisture levels; make sure soil is well drained. Do not mulch cherries; just mow the grass. Mulching will slow down the fruit and encourage disease. Cherries need little pruning and little fertiliser; too much nitrogen will also encourage fruit to split. A scatter of blood and bone or old hen manure once a year on the mown grass should be sufficient.

WOOD-BURROWING MOTHS
Symptoms: Holes in the trunk, usually seen after the larvae have left. Sawdust deposits indicate that moths may still be present.
Solution: Prise them out of their holes with a piece of wire, or inject some insecticide into the hole. Fill holes with grafting wax or putty.

CHESTNUT

See Walnut, p. 17.

CITRUS

APHIDS
Symptoms: Small sap-suckers on new shoots.
Solution: See Avocado, p. 61.

BLACK SPOT

Symptoms: Sunken brown or black spots on fruit.
Solution: See Brown or septoria spot below.

BROWN CENTRES

These are caused by a boron deficiency, possibly precipitated by dry or very wet weather.
Solution: Improve the feeding regime and in the short-term spray liquid fertiliser as a foliar spray.

BROWN OR SEPTORIA SPOT

Symptoms: Clusters of small brown spots joined together, often after autumn rain.
Solution: See Brown rot under Apricot, p. 60.

COLLAR ROT

Symptoms: Tree dies back; yellowed foliage; lifted bark at base of tree.
Solution: Cut back all dead wood and bark; paint with Bordeaux paste. Make sure new trees are planted with the bud union at least 10 cm above ground level. Keep grass and mulch at least 10 cm back from the trunk. This will prevent moisture collecting there and injury to the tree from close mowing.

DEFORMED FRUIT

Symptoms: Fruit is folded into many sections or into other strange shapes.
Solution: This is caused by citrus bud mites, tiny insects that feed in unopened leaf and flower buds. They are worst on Eureka lemons and Washington Navel oranges. Hot, dry weather is usually enough to control them. In cool, moist weather dust with sulphur, or spray with wettable sulphur when the first symptoms become visible.

DRY CENTRES

This may be caused by citrus bug (see p. 65) or lack of water.

FAILURE TO FRUIT

Solution: Citrus trees may not fruit for about three years. If they are still not fruiting after that, they may have been fed too much nitrogen in proportion to phosphorous. Establish a good regime of compost/mulch/blood and bone or old hen manure; dress with ground rock phosphorous meanwhile. Encourage a good bee population for pollination and protect against possible frosts at flowering time (see Frost, pp. 21–23). Fruit drop may occur if the soil has too much nitrogen, not enough or fluctuating water, or if there is poor pollination or more than 3 thrips per flower.

FRUIT FLY

Symptoms: Small puncture holes within round, brownish patches, followed by rotting fruit with maggots.
Solution: See Fruit fly, pp. 53–56.

GALL WASPS

Symptoms: Round galls (abnormal outgrowths) on branches, produced by the tunnelling larvae of gall wasps.
Solution: Cut out galls and burn them before the end of winter so they cannot hatch and worsen the problem; encourage bird, ant and spider predators.

LEMON SCAB

Symptoms: Misshapen or 'horned' fruit with scabby tops.
Solution: This is caused by a fungus attacking the fruit soon after it is set. At petal fall spray with Bordeaux and experiment with a spray of 1 part urine to 9 parts water. Feed trees with compost or good mulch, especially rotten lucerne or comfrey leaves, or wattle bark mixed with slashed wattle leaf. Well-fed trees are more resistant to scab.

Note: scab-like symptoms can also be caused by cold damage or stink bug damage.

PREMATURE FRUIT DROP

Symptons: Most citrus lose some of their crop; this makes the rest fatter.

Solution: If the garden is subject to strong, dry winds, try to establish windbreaks. Mulch well so that trees do not suffer moisture stress.

RED SCALE
Symptoms: Small red scabs over fruit.
Solution: Use sprays which kill wasp parasites. See Scale, pp. 115–16.

PHYTOPHTHORA AND OTHER ROOT ROTS
Symptoms: Foliage starts to die, often on one side only; tree dies back; foliage yellows and dulls.
Solution: Use trifoliata rootstock, which is resistant to phytophthora root rot. In bad cases cut the tree back to healthy wood and feed the tree with a foliar spray until the root system can reestablish itself. Be warned: the rot may be controlled with compost, but in wet years, or if the compost regime is not continued, the tree may start to die back again. Exercise vigilance once symptoms appear.

Be wary of wattle tree roots growing near citrus; they can harbour root rots. If wattle trees are cut down, make sure all the roots are removed and the hole is left open to the sun for several weeks. See Root rots, pp. 56–57.

RUSTY FRUIT
This is caused by harmless citrus rust mites feeding on the skin and does not affect the fruit itself. Mites are prevalent in humid or coastal areas; hot, dry weather usually controls them.

SOOTY BLACK FRUIT
See Sooty mould, pp. 116–17.

STINK, HORNED AND OTHER BUGS
Symptoms: These sap-suckers are oval or shield-shaped. Stink bugs smell; they also emit an acrid fluid that can sting. Shoots and even branches may wilt with infestation and the tree becomes generally unthrifty.
Solution: Interplant scented climbing geraniums to control stink bugs. This works well. Make sure all ripe fruit is picked and all fallen fruit is removed. The scent of rotting or ripe fruit attracts stink bugs.

Control weeds around the trees by mulching, weeding or slashing. Clear away old pots, wood heaps and old fences that may harbour colonies near trees. Reflective foil mulches around the trees should deter the adults. The bugs are predated by a range of parasitic fungi, wasps, birds, ladybirds, lacewings and hoverfly larvae.

• Spray with bug juice.

• Pick off the bugs by hand (*wear gloves* for stink bugs).

• Place cardboard shelters or bits of old hose around the infected plants. The bugs may shelter there during the day. Check them daily.

• Hose trees with as strong a jet as possible, especially under the leaves, or shake the trees. Pick up and squash fallen bugs.

• As a last resort, try quassia, wormwood, rhubarb leaf or diatomaceous earth sprays. These will be effective for a few days; if the trees are being recolonised with bugs from elsewhere, the sprays will appear not to work. Other measures above must be used in conjunction with the spray to prevent large-scale reinfection.

THICK RIND
Solution: This is common in young fruit trees and should lessen as they get older. Overripe Valencia oranges also have a thick rind. Thick rind occurs naturally in some varieties. It may also be caused by cold weather. In older trees thick skin can indicate excess nitrogen. Add some ground rock phosphate as a temporary measure and stick to good quality mulches with a little added blood and bone or hen manure as a feeding regime.

CURRANT

BIRDS
Solution: See Birds, p. 44. Try stringing up black cotton as a mini bird net or cover the fruit with old pantyhose stretched on wire loops.

BUD OR GALL MITE
Symptoms: Enlarged and distorted buds that fail to develop.
Solution: Spray with Bordeaux in winter; cut off distorted buds and burn them; spray the rest of the plant with double-strength garlic spray or elder spray.

CURRANT BORER
Symptoms: Caterpillars bore into the stems causing them to wilt and die off.
Solution: Cut off the stems and burn them; other control is difficult as borers are protected inside the stems.

EELWORM
Symptoms: Shrivelled, dark buds.
Solution: Remove and burn affected buds; make sure plants are well mulched, preferably with compost. A healthy population of earthworms is the best defense.

FAILURE TO SET FRUIT
Currants have a high chilling requirement. Mild winters mean no fruit.

PALE FOLIAGE
Solution: Currants need high potash levels. Sprinkle with wood ash every year and mulch with compost, lucerne or manure. Black currants need more nitrogen than red and white currants; so they should have well-rotted hen manure or blood and bone every year unless compost is used.

SEPTORIA LEAF ROT AND OTHER FUNGAL DISEASES
Solution: Spray with Bordeaux when dormant; use chamomile tea, elder spray, casuarina spray or milk spray when in leaf. Pick off leaves at first symptoms and burn or hot-compost.

CUSTARD APPLE

BUGS
Symptoms: Water-soaked blotching on fruit. See Citrus for prevention and control, p. 65.

FRUIT FLY
Symptoms: Brownish spots around small holes in the fruit.
Solution: See Fruit fly, pp. 53–56.

FEIJOA

BLACK SCALE
See Scale, pp. 115–16.

FAILURE TO FRUIT
Solution: Feijoas need two trees for pollination, although occasionally one tree grown alone will fruit.

FRUIT FLY
Solution: Feijoa has a reputation for attracting fruit fly with its particularly strong scent. Autumn ripening means it is particularly vulnerable. Use traps and practise garden hygiene: see Fruit fly, pp. 53–56.

TASTELESS FRUIT
Let the feijoas ripen fully on the tree, then fall to the ground; this will also help soften the fruit.

FIG

BIRDS
See Birds, p. 44.

BORER MOTHS
Symptoms: Sawdust, holes in trunk and branches (these may be noticeable only after the borer has left).

Solution: Push out borers with a bit of fuse wire or inject pyrethrum; then fill holes with Bordeaux paste or putty. Bordeaux spray or wood ash and water spray will stop the moths laying eggs. If borers are a recurring problem, prune back the tree to encourage new, resistant growth.

FAILURE TO FRUIT
Solution: Figs need very little pruning, although they fruit on new wood; enough usually grows each year. If old trees stop fruiting, cut them back well in winter.

LATE SECOND CROP
Solution: If fruit may be burnt by frost, wrap them in sacking on the tree. If fruit are clearly not going to ripen, remove them, as they may inhibit the next crop.

SPLIT FRUIT
This is worst in humid or coastal areas, because figs prefer low humidity. Figs will also split with alternating dry and wet soil. In humid areas, avoid fertilising figs at all; the fruit may be small, but it is more likely to be whole.

GOOSEBERRY

CATERPILLARS
Solution: Try dilute clay spray, pikelet spray, dusted rock phosphate (on leaves) or white pepper spray; as a last resort use Dipel, garlic, derris or pyrethrum sprays.

FUNGAL PROBLEMS: POWDERY MILDEW, GREY MOULD, ETC.
Symptoms: Fungal problems on foliage.
Solution: Spray with Bordeaux when dormant. Carefully prune the tops of bushes to let in air and light. Spray leaves with chamomile tea, or elder or casuarina sprays.

MITES
Symptoms: Leaves may become yellow, webbed or dried out. Mites are too small to be seen clearly by the naked eye, but droppings may be visible.
Solution: See Red spider mite under Apple, p. 59.

GRAPEFRUIT

See Citrus, pp. 61–65.

PREMATURE FRUIT DROP
Solution: Grapefruit are prone to this. Avoid fluctuations in soil moisture and mulch heavily. Fruit drop may simply be due to more fruit setting than the tree can sustain.

GRAPE

FAILURE TO FRUIT
Grapes bear on growth from last season's wood; failure to fruit can be caused by pruning too heavily. Powdery mildew may affect flowers. Wasps can also suck out the centre of the fruit; birds and possums can eat the immature fruit.
Solution: Spray with Bordeaux in winter. See Birds, p. 44 and Possums, p. 47.

FUNGAL, MOULD AND MILDEW DISEASES
Symptoms: Rotting or withered fruit; powdery deposits on vines; falling flowers that fail to fruit.
Solution: See Brown rot under Apricot, p. 60.

LIGHT BROWN APPLE MOTH AND OTHER MOTHS
Solution: See Light brown apple moth, under Apple, p. 59 for controls.

MEALY AND RUTHERGLEN BUGS
Solution: Mow and mulch for weed control and encourage predators. A reflective foil mulch may deter them. See Citrus, p. 65 for traps and sprays.

MITES
Symptoms: Webbed, yellow or dry leaves.

Solution: See Gooseberry, p. 67, and Red spider mite under Apple, p. 59.

PHYLLOXERA

Symptoms: This is an aphid that forms galls on the roots of the plants, greatly reducing vigour and eventually killing them. Its spread is so far limited in Australia.

Solution: Be careful taking cuttings if the area may be affected — contact the Department of Agriculture to find out what areas are affected. Grow vines from resistant stock. See Aphids under Avocado, p. 61.

UNEVEN RIPENING

This can be caused by lack of pruning: the vine may be carrying more fruit than it can cope with. Sometimes fluctuating temperatures can cause uneven ripening.

Solution: Prune regularly.

VINE AND ELEPHANT WEEVILS

Symptoms: Tunnels in canes.

Solution: Cut out and burn affected canes.

VIRAL DISEASES

Symptoms: Grapes are subject to a range of viral diseases; there is no cure. Look for reddish-purple blotches between the leaves, yellow mottling and deformed canes. Call the Department of Agriculture for verification then dig out affected canes at once and burn them.

HAZELNUT

APHIDS

Symptoms: Small insects clustered on new shoots.

Solution: See Avocado, p. 61.

BIRDS

See Birds, p. 44.

MILDEW AND HAZELNUT BLIGHT

Solution: These leaf diseases can be controlled with Bordeaux spray in winter.

Mulch well and do not interplant. Hedged plants result in increased retention of leaf litter, which forms a natural mulch. This is one situation where crowded trees are less prone to blight than well-spaced ones.

KIWI FRUIT

BIRDS

Solution: Raise the pergolas slightly higher than the vines and net them. See Birds, p. 44.

FAILURE TO FRUIT

Solution: Kiwi fruit need male and female vines to set fruit. Intertwine the male and female vines, especially during cool, damp springs when bees may be scarce. Kiwi fruit grow on year-old wood, so over-heavy pruning may reduce the next fruit crop.

LIGHT BROWN APPLE MOTH AND OTHER MOTHS

Symptoms: Caterpillars damage leaves and fruit.

Solution: See Apple, p. 59.

MEALY AND RUTHERGLEN BUG

See Citrus, p. 65.

LEMON

See Citrus, pp. 61–65.

ROUGH LEMONS

Symptons: These may grow from the original stock below the graft of the citrus. The fruit is rounder and more orange than most lemons, knobbly, with thick rinds.

Solution: Cut them out and regraft, or leave them to fruit; the fruit is of poor quality but useable and incredibly hardy.

LIME

See Citrus, pp. 61–65.

These are more frost-tender than lemons and live only about fifteen years. Mulch well to increase life span. Pick limes when they are still light green, before they start fall off the tree; bright yellow limes are overripe.

MELANOSE

Symptoms: Fruit is scabby and leaves develop brown blotches within yellowy patches. Limes are more subject to melanose than other citrus.
Solution: Spray with Bordeaux at petal fall. Cut out all dead twigs, remove all weeds near the trees and mulch heavily, renewing the mulch at least every six months.

LOQUAT

BIENNIAL BEARING

Solution: Thin the crop each year to even out production. Many loquats are, however, naturally biennial.

BIRDS

See Birds, p. 44.

FRUIT FLY

Symptoms: Small brown patches on fruit; maggots inside.
Solution: Use traps and hygiene. See Fruit fly, pp. 53–56.

NON-BEARING TREES

Seedling loquats can take fifteen years to bear.
Solution: Grafting is a possibility.

SCAB

Symptoms: Raised, scabby spots on fruit.
Solution: Spray with half-strength Bordeaux in autumn, or at any time with a spray of 1 part urine to 9 parts chamomile tea water to stop the condition spreading. Some fruit thinning may be necessary.

LYCHEE

CRACKED FRUIT

Solution: Fruit may crack in areas with low humidity. Keep the area crowded with foliage. Use microjets or sprinklers to keep up humidity.

FRUIT BATS

Solution: Try nets and tape-recorded loud noises. See Fruit bats, p. 45.

FRUIT FLY

See Fruit fly, pp. 53–56.

MITES

Symptoms: Blossom drop; small, red, felt-like patches under leaves.
Solution: See Gooseberry, p. 67.

MACADAMIA

BORER

Symptoms: Sawdust deposits on branches or the ground; new shoots die.
Solution: See Fig, pp. 67–68.

FAILURE TO FRUIT

Seedling trees may not bear for ten to fifteen years, especially in cooler areas. Blossom may also be attacked by a range of pests.
Solution: See Attracting predators, pp. 6–7.

NUT BORER

Symptoms: Fruit are webbed, holed, or fall prematurely.
Solution: Natural predators should keep this pest in check. Try a light Bordeaux spray.

PHYTOPHTHORA AND OTHER ROOT ROTS

Symptoms: Symptoms are like those of collar rot. See Collar rot under Citrus, p. 64.
Solution: Mulch with the wattle bark, comfrey and lucerne compost described under Root rots, pp. 56–57, or with lucerne hay with a little dolomite; cut out affected areas and paint with Bordeaux to prevent other infections; grow only in well-drained soils and keep up levels of organic matter in the soil.

MANDARIN

See Citrus, pp. 61–65.

BIENNIAL BEARING

Solution: Thin out very heavy crops while still small and green; in light fruit years, leave some fruit on the tree. This will inhibit fruit formation in the next heavy-bearing year.

DRY AND TASTELESS FRUIT

These have been left too long on the tree. Not all citrus is orange when it is ripe; the taste test is the only reliable one. Some varieties of mandarin are only bright orange when overripe.

MANGO

ANTHRACNOSE STEM END ROT

Symptoms: Blackened, rotten fruit and peel at the stalk end of the fruit, which may encroach upwards into the fruit.
Solution: Pick fruit with stem on. Do not twist, or the join may be damaged.

FAILURE TO FRUIT

Wet conditions at flowering time often cause fungus-induced blossom rot.
Solution: Spray with chamomile, casuarina or chive tea after rainstorms but no more than once every two days. Prune off all dead wood.

FRUIT FLY

Symptoms: Small brown sting marks on the fruit; maggots inside.
Solution: See Fruit fly, pp. 53–56.

POWDERY MILDEW

Symptoms: Powdery deposits on leaves.
Solution: See Brown rot under Apricot, p. 60.

SOOTY MOULD ON FOLIAGE

Symptoms: Black, sooty patches.
Solution: See Sooty mould, pp. 116–17.

MEDLAR

CRACKED FRUIT

Solution: This is due to heavy or prolonged rain. Improve drainage, if necessary; do not feed with soluble nitrogenous fertilisers.

FRUIT FLY

Solution: See Fruit fly, pp. 53–56. Medlars are hard fruit that can be left to ripen indoors where they will be relatively free of fruit fly.

MULBERRY

BACTERIAL BLIGHT

Symptoms: Leaves develop brown spots, often with a spreading yellow halo. Young shoots may die back.
Solution: See Brown rot under Apricot, p. 60.

CANKER

Symptoms: Dark, splitting bark, dead wood.
Solution: Avoid pruning where possible as canker usually enters by pruning wounds. If pruning is essential, spray the dormant tree with Bordeaux just before pruning, and respray the wound just after pruning.

COLLAR ROT

Symptoms: Dead bark and wood at ground level.
Solution: Mulberries are prone to collar rot. Keep mulch away from the trunk. Grass mowings and an occasional scattering of blood and bone are sufficient care for a mulberry. Do not mow too close to the tree trunk; collar rot may start from lawnmower wounds. Sow gazanias or other ground covers around the trunk so that mowing is not necessary.

NECTARINE

See Peach, pp. 72–73.

OLIVE

BROWN OLIVE SCALE

Symptoms: Brownish, scaly patches on foliage.

Solution: Brown scale is usually controlled by predators. Try jetting it off with water if it is really damaging the tree or use a light oil spray if the temperature is below 24°C. See Scale, pp. 115–16.

LACK OF FRUIT

This may be because the plant is the African (not European) olive, which will bear fruit no larger than a small pea. The African is the common hedging olive, and has become a major weed in some areas. It has glossier foliage than the European olive and a yellowish tinge to new growth on the back of the leaves, while the European olive has bluish-grey new growth.

Fruit may also not set in humid areas with warm winters. Olives like cold winters and hot, dry summers. Old trees may also become unproductive. This may be cured by hard cutting back and feeding well.

SUCKERS

These can be caused by heavy pruning or too much nitrogen in the soil, or they may occur simply because the variety is prone to suckering. Seedling suckers will produce fruit as good as that from the main tree. If you wish to remove suckers, slice them out with a sharp spade or other implement.

ORANGE

See Citrus, pp. 61–65.

GREEN COLOURED VALENCIAS

Solution: Valencia oranges do not turn bright orange like artificially treated commercially grown fruit until they are overripe. By this time the skins are puffy and the fruit is not as sweet to eat.

PASSIONFRUIT

CRINKLY SKIN

This is caused by dry soil. Often crinkly-skinned passionfruit are the sweetest.

FAILURE TO SET FRUIT

This can happen in hot, dry summers when the pollen dries out, or in very humid conditions, when blossoms rot. Too much nitrogen at the expense of phosphorous can lead to poor fruit set or few blossoms.

Solution: Add some ground rock phosphate and prune back new growth.

FRUIT FLY

Symptoms: Fruit fly may sting green fruit. The larvae usually do not penetrate the fruit; they merely leave a scabby patch on the skin. See Fruit fly, pp. 53–56.

FUSARIUM WILT

Symptoms: The vine suddenly wilts, rotting the stem of the plant at ground level.

Solution: Prevent fusarium wilt by only planting passionfruit grafted onto resistant stock or by covering the ground with clear plastic for three weeks before the vine is planted.

Vigorously growing vines are more resistant. Prune older vines back each year to encourage new growth and keep feeding well with good compost and a scatter of pelletised or old hen manure, or blood and bone. Wood ash or compost will give the soil added potash for greater resistance to fusarium wilt.

If the vine is attacked, paint the base of the stem with Bordeaux paste, and spray the soil around the plant with double-strength garlic spray. The best solution, however, is simply to remove the vine and plant another somewhere else. Do not plant a vine where an infected vine has been for at least three years, and soak the ground with garlic spray first. Healthy passionfruit will fruit in their first year.

GREEN SHIELD BUGS

Symptoms: These suck the fruit, causing a raised scabbiness or a thin, shell-like patch.
Solution: See Citrus, pp. 61–65.

PASSION VINE HOPPERS

Symptoms: These are small brown moths with partially transparent wings, which lay eggs in the vine shoots where suffocating sprays cannot get to them. Leaves wilt, fruit shrivels, and honeydew, with possible sooty mould, grows on the excretions of the hopper.
Solution: Cut off affected shoots; spray with pyrethrum, derris or garlic spray.

PREMATURE FRUIT DROP

This may be due to dry soil or to frost.
Solution: Mulch well and water. See Frost, pp. 21–23.

WOODY PASSIONFRUIT

Symptoms: Do not confuse this with cold damage, which causes empty fruit. Woody passionfruit have a thickened rind, whereas cold-damaged fruit do not. Fruit is dry and leaves may be a mottled yellow.
Solution: There is no cure for this virus, but strongly growing vines are less susceptible. Dig out infected vines and do not replant passionfruit there. Be careful that secateurs are not infected; dip them in vinegar or boiling water before use.

PAW PAW

FAILURE TO FRUIT

Most paw paws need male and female trees to set fruit. Bisexual trees may revert to single-sex in cool conditions. Male flowers have a long stalk; females look stumpier, and the somewhat larger flowers are reproduced in the leaf axil.

DIEBACK

Symptoms: Tree dies back from the top.

Solution: The exact cause of this common problem is unknown. Cut the plant at a healthy spot.

POWDERY MILDEW

Symptoms: Powdery leaves.
Solution: Spray wettable sulphur under and on top of the leaves. Powdery mildew is worse in cool weather and should correct itself as the days warm up. The fruit is usually still edible, so in most cases just wait for the problem to correct itself.

PEACH

BACTERIAL GUMMOSIS

Symptoms: Gum exudes from trunk or branches.
Solution: Spray with Bordeaux in winter, especially before or after pruning. Feed trees with compost or good mulch, especially rotten lucerne or comfrey leaves. Well-fed trees are more resistant to bacterial gummosis.

BREAKING BRANCHES

Solution: Peach wood is brittle, so heavily laden branches may need support to prevent breaking. Prop them up with wooden stakes or loop with rope to the main trunk. Avoid radical 'vase-shaped' pruning.

BROWN ROT

Symptoms: Brown or powdery rot on fruit.
Solution: See Apricot, p. 60.

CANKER

Symptoms: Dark, cracking bark, dead wood.
Solution: See Cherry, p. 63.

CURLY LEAF

Symptoms: Pink or green blisters on leaves. Eventually the young shoots die. If untreated, bad cases of curly leaf can gradually weaken the whole tree.

Solution: This can be prevented but there is no way to get rid of the pink blisters once they have formed. They are unsightly but not harmful.

Spray peach trees with Bordeaux at leaf fall and bud swell if they, or nearby trees, have been previously infected with curly leaf. For mild cases, spray once only, between leaf fall and bud swell. Unfortunately the same fungus can also cause premature fruit drop. If the curly leaf is affecting new leaves, or young shoots are dying back, pick off all affected leaves and spray the tree weekly with chamomile tea, casuarina tea or horsetail tea for three weeks.

Curly leaf is worst in wet years. Planting garlic thickly under the trees may help to inhibit curly leaf.

FAILURE TO FRUIT

This may be caused by curly leaf (see above). The trees may also not have had enough chilling, or the blossom may have been affected by late frosts. The J. H. Hale variety also needs cross-pollination. Possums, parrots and rosellas love to eat blossom. See Possums, p. 47 and Birds, p. 44.

FRUIT DROP

This is usually because of fruit fly infection. See Fruit fly, pp. 53–56.

PEACH RUST

Symptoms: Brown spots on leaves.
Solution: Spray with Bordeaux when dormant.

VIRUSES

Peaches are susceptible to a wide range of viruses. Look for unusual leaf or growth patterns.
Solution: There is no cure but it is said that regular treatment with seaweed spray makes trees more resistant to viruses.

PEAR

FRUIT DROP

Solution: Avoid dry soil; ensure varieties pollinate each other. (To check this, cut open a dropped pear; if there are fewer seeds than normal, it probably has not been pollinated.) Grow flowers to attract bees; install bee hives; check that neighbours are not using bee-killing pesticides.

FRUIT ROTS

Solution: These are usually caused when fruit is bruised in picking. Handle carefully.

MITES

See Gooseberry, p. 67.

PEAR AND CHERRY SLUG

Symptoms: Slug-like sawfly larvae make web-like patterns on leaves. In bad cases the tree may be defoliated.
Solution: See Cherry, p. 63.

SCALE

See pp. 115–16.

PECANS

BIRDS

See Birds, p. 44.

PREMATURE FRUIT FALL

Solution: Avoid fluctuating moisture levels; fruit fall may be caused by inadequate feeding. Pecan scab causes premature fruit fall but so far has been kept out of Australia. Pecans naturally fall from the tree when they are ripe. This avoids the need to pick.

WOOD BORER, PEACH MOTH BORER

Symptoms: These bore into the nuts.
Solution: Follow controls for Codling moth pp. 51–53. Feed trees with compost or good mulch; mulches made from rotten lucerne or comfrey leaves are especially effective.

PERSIMMON

ASTRINGENT FRUIT
Older varieties are often more astringent.

FAILURE TO SET FRUIT
Solution: Most modern persimmon varieties are self-pollinating. Some older varieties, however, require a male plant for fertilisation. A dry spring or excess nitrogen can impair fruiting. Apparent failure to fruit may also be caused by birds eating the fruit soon after fruit set; see Birds, p. 44.

FRUIT FLY
Solution: Persimmons are usually only subject to fruit fly in warm areas where fruit fly survive through winter. See Fruit fly, pp. 53–56.

PREMATURE FRUIT DROP
Solution: This may be caused by dryness, fluctuating moisture levels, or pruning.

ROOT ROTS
Solution: Plant in well-drained soils. See Root rots, pp. 56–57.

PINEAPPLE

MEALY BUGS
Symptoms: Tiny wax-covered ovals on leaves; leaves and shoots wilt; mealy bug secretions encourage sooty mould.
Solution: Control the ants that bring the mealy bugs by applying grease bands at the base of the tree; encourage ladybirds, lacewing larvae and chalcid parasitic wasps. Prune affected foliage if possible; use oil sprays if the temperature is below 24°C or soapy water in the cool of the evening. Avoid common insecticides: they are not effective, as they do not penetrate mealy bugs' protective coating.

NEMATODES
Symptoms: Slow-growing, stunted plants that wilt in hot weather.
Solution: Try a good companion crop of mustard all around the plants. Grow a green manure crop of millet, broad beans, etc. and slash it, rather than dig it in, then scatter on sulphate of ammonia to help speed up decomposition. Mulch constantly and keep up levels of organic matter, especially in sandy soil. The mycelium webs in compost will inhibit harmful nematodes. So will a large population of earthworms. Keep soil bare for three months before replanting.

ROOT ROTS
Solution: Ensure good drainage, and mulch; keep plants growing strongly. See Phytophthora under Avocado, p. 62.

PISTACHIO

FAILURE TO FRUIT
Pistachios need male and female trees to fruit. They also need hot, dry summers and cold winters. They may fail to fruit in humid, wet or hot areas.

PLUM

BACTERIAL SPOT
Symptoms: Light green spots on leaves, small, scabby, cracked spots on fruit.
Solution: Spray Bordeaux at bud swell and use elder or chamomile sprays on foliage to stop the problem spreading.

BROWN ROT
Symptoms: Brown, rotten patches on fruit.
Solution: See Apricot, p. 60.

FRUIT FLY
See Fruit fly, pp. 53–56.

GUMMOSIS
Symptoms: Gum is exuded from trunk or branches.
Solution: Spray with Bordeaux when dormant.

LIGHT BROWN APPLE MOTH
Solution: See Apple, p. 59.

MITES
Symptoms: Distorted foliage or flowers; small, black droppings.
Solution: See Gooseberry, p. 67.

PEAR AND CHERRY SLUG
Symptoms: Slug-like sawfly larvae skeletonise the leaves.
Solution: See Cherry, p. 63.

PRUNE RUST
Symptoms: Powdery brown spots under the leaves.
Solution: Spray with Bordeaux at bud swell.

SAN JOSÉ SCALE
Symptoms: Scale-like encrustations on the leaves.
Solution: See Scale, pp. 115–16.

SHOT HOLE
Symptoms: Small holes in the leaves.
Solution: Spray with Bordeaux at bud swell. See Brown rot under Apricot, p. 60.

SILVER LEAF
Symptoms: Plums are very susceptible to silver leaf, a wood-rotting fungus. This releases a toxin that travels through the tree. The leaves turn silvery and branch after branch may die.
Solution: There is no conventional cure. An old remedy is to slit the bark of the tree with a pruning knife down through the outside layer and into the wood. This should be done in winter for up to four years.
   Silver leaf is best prevented by not pruning in wet weather, and by covering all cuts with a Bordeaux paste or spraying with Bordeaux just before or after pruning.

PLUMCOT

This is a cross between a plum and an apricot. See Plum, pp. 74–75 and Apricot, pp. 60–61.

POMEGRANATE

SPLITTING FRUIT
Fruit splits in wet weather or if it is overripe. If necessary, pick fruit while it is still yellow and let it ripen indoors.

QUINCE

CODLING MOTH
See Codling moth, pp. 51–53.

FRUIT FLY
See Fruit fly, pp. 53–56.

ORIENTAL PEACH MOTH
See Peach, pp. 72–73.

QUINCE FLECK
Symptoms: This is a fungus disease which results in black spots on leaves and cracked fruit.
Solution: Train trees to a single open-branched stem so that light can penetrate. Do not plant quinces in a humid, sheltered spot e.g. near a fish pond or an often-watered vegetable garden. See Brown rot under Apricot, p. 60.

RASPBERRY, LOGANBERRY, YOUNGBERRY, BOYSENBERRY

APHIDS
Symptoms: Clusters of small insects on new shoots.
Solution: See Scale, pp. 115–16 .

CANE SPOT

Symptoms: Purple spots on canes.
Solution: Spray with Bordeaux at mid-winter or half-strength Bordeaux at bud swell. A spray of 1 soluble aspirin to 2 cups warm water may help. Regular treatments with seaweed or nettle spray may encourage some resistance.

DOWNY MILDEW

Symptoms: Powdery deposits on leaves.
Solution: See Cane spot, above. Treat with chamomile or garlic sprays when canes have foliage. Cut out affected leaves at first symptoms. Fungus and mildews will be better prevented if canes are grown in thick lucerne, comfrey mulch or compost and not boosted into sudden, sappy growth by excesses of nitrogen and water.

HARD RASPBERRIES

Solution: These may have been sucked by harlequin beetles. Thin out vines and clear away debris that may be sheltering the beetles. A band of turnips can act as a decoy crop for harlequin beetles. A reflective aluminium foil mulch may keep the beetles away. So will individual collars (for each cane) made from sharp bits of soft drink bottle; or try a thick splodge of tree-banding grease. See Stink, horned and other bugs under Citrus, p. 65.

LIGHT BROWN APPLE MOTH

See Apple, p. 59.

MITES

Symptoms: Yellow, pale, mottled or dry leaves.
Solution: See Apple, p. 59.

MOULDY RASPBERRIES

Solution: As this is common after rain, pick ripe raspberries as soon as the rain stops; remove mouldy ones to stop them infecting others and spray the rest with chamomile tea. Avoid water-soluble, high-nitrogen fertilisers.

Feed raspberries a good mulch of lucerne or compost, frequently renewed.

RASPBERRY LEAF RUST

Symptoms: Rusty patches on canes.
Solution: See Cane spot, above.

SPUR BLIGHT

Symptoms: Silver-brown fungus on canes.
Solution: See Cane spot, above.

THRIPS

Symptoms: Distorted leaves or flowers; premature petal drop; small, black droppings.
Solution: See Apple, pp. 59–60.

STRAWBERRY

APHIDS

Symptoms: Clusters of insects on new shoots.
Solution: See Scale, pp. 115–16.

BIRDS, SLUGS AND SNAILS

See Birds, p. 44, and Slugs and snails, pp. 48–49.

BOTRYTIS

Symptoms: Soft, watery, pale berries that appear almost rotten.
Solution: This fungus thrives in moist, sheltered areas. Prune off some of the foliage, especially if it might have been stimulated by too much nitrogen-rich fertiliser. Spray with half-strength Bordeaux late at night; use chamomile tea spray any time.

EELWORMS

Symptoms: These inch their way into the fruit and hollow it out.
Solution: Eelworms like very ripe strawberries. Pick fruit every day. Mulch with compost or chopped mustard and marigold leaves and flowers; this discourages eelworm. The best defense is a heavy earthworm population. In very bad cases, as a temporary solution only, use a weed mat with horto paper or old newspaper mulch.

Ichneumonoids are useful parasites and help control caterpillars, slugs and sawfly larvae.

Mealy bugs are difficult to kill because of their protective coating. They are attracted to plants by the sticky substances which ants transfer, so control the ants by spraying them thoroughly with white oil.

Good garden design can help combat a range of environmental problems.
This terraced garden grown above heat-absorbent paving is protected against frost damage.

Inexpensive and effective organic remedies can be made from ingredients found in your kitchen cupboard.

LEAF-SPOTTING DISEASES

Solution: Several leaf-spotting diseases attack strawberries; all require the same preventive measures and treatment. Mulch strawberries thickly, and avoid overhead watering; use drippers or a hose poked under the mulch. In bad cases, thin out leaves to improve air and light penetration. A half-strength Bordeaux mixture can be used when cropping has finished for the year. Otherwise, spray weeds with chamomile spray or seaweed spray. Feed plants with compost or good mulch, especially rotten lucerne or comfrey leaves or well-rotted wattle bark and leaves. Well-fed plants are more resistant to leaf spot.

NEMATODES

Symptoms: Plants may suddenly die.
Solution: Grow a crop of mustard before strawberries are planted; this will discourage nematodes. Use compost (nematodes are inhibited by the mycelium webs); keep up organic matter by mulching, especially in sandy soils. Make sure soil is rich in earthworms.

RED SPIDER MITES

Symptoms: Dull, pitted-looking leaves.
Solution: Spray on top and under foliage with milk spray; see Apple, p. 59.

(Note: another mite species, the two-spotted mite, is sometimes confused with rust. The two-spotted mite causes the leaves to turn rusty brown with a fine lacy webbing underneath. Look for this webbing.)

TAMARILLO

FRUIT FLY

See Fruit fly, pp. 53–56.

ROOT ROTS

Symptoms: Plants may suddenly or gradually wilt and die.
Solution: See Phytophthora, p. 62.

TANGELO

These are a cross between a mandarin and a grapefruit. See Citrus, pp. 61–65.

WALNUT

BACTERIAL BLIGHT

Symptoms: Black spots on leaves, black, withered nuts inside.
Solution: Spray with Bordeaux in winter, or at leaf fall and bud swell for bad cases.

BIRDS

See Birds, p. 44.

ROOT ROTS

A number of root rots affect walnuts. Leaves and branches die from the tips down. Ensure good drainage and make sure there are no native trees nearby from which shoelace fungus can be transferred. See Root rots, pp. 56–57.

CHAPTER SEVEN

VEGETABLES

PROBLEMS

For individual spray recipes, refer to Chapter Four, Organic Remedies (or see index).

AMARANTH

LODGING

Symptoms: Plants fall over in wet weather.

Solution: Grow in a sheltered spot. Do not force-feed with too much nitrogen. Grow where a well-manured crop has grown before; no other feeding is then necessary. A coarse mulch such as tossed-up lucerne hay will offer some support.

ARTICHOKE (GLOBE)

LEAF-EATING LADYBIRDS

Symptoms: These have 28 spots and are not to be confused with other valuable predator ladybirds.

Solution: Sprinkle the leaves with diatomaceous earth or use a talcum powder spray: add water to talcum powder and drizzle it over the leaves. This will both repel and kill the ladybirds. If the infestation is bad enough to stunt the plant (which is unlikely), sprinkle the leaves with derris, or use a derris or pyrethrum spray on the leaves, not on the pest itself. Stomach poisons such as derris are more effective than contact poisons.

TOUGH OR SPIKY ARTICHOKES

Solution: Pick the artichoke earlier. Some varieties are spikier than others, and some seedlings may have reverted to a spiky form.

BROAD BEAN

APHIDS

Symptoms: Shiny, black insects clustered on the tips; twisted leaves.

Solution: Broad bean aphids are worst when the crop has been planted too late or too early, and either late autumn pests or early spring pests attack the plants. Most aphid plagues will be controlled naturally as soon as the predators become active, a week or two after the aphids.

In long, cool, unseasonal springs the aphid infestation may linger.

Pick the tips of each plant, shake off the aphids or squash them, or spray with soapy water. (The broad bean tips can be cooked like silver beet.) Try reflective aluminium foil mulch between rows. In bad cases, treat with marigold or pyrethrum spray.

BROAD BEAN WILT

Symptoms: Tips become black and die. Dieback may continue down the plant; stems may also be black and rotten at ground level.
Solution: This is a virus. Remove infected plants at once and control aphids, which spread the disease. The virus is worst in cold weather; plants may recover once the temperature is over 20°C. Careful tilling of crops may help control a persistent problem.

CATERPILLARS

Solution: Try a tansy antifeedant spray; use pikelet spray or dust with white pepper. In bad cases use Dipel combined with regular picking of the pods. See Brassicas, p. 80–83.

CHOCOLATE SPOT

Symptoms: Dark brown to black spots or dieback on the leaves.
Solution: Add wood ash or compost or comfrey mulch to provide potash. Spray with garlic spray made with soapy water as soon as first spots appear. Repeat every few days, especially in rainy weather. Crop rotate with garlic. Compost-fed plants are more resistant to chocolate spot.

LODGING

Symptoms: Plants fall down and rot.
Solution: Grow a dwarf variety. Plant the beans close together in a mass, or in rows three abreast, or in the centre of a ring of chicken wire so they get some support; a coarse lucerne hay mulch will also help. In windy areas, grow them with a windbreak of old corn stalks or a trellis of climbing peas.

RUST

Symptoms: Brown velvet pustules on leaves.
Solution: Mulch, and avoid overhead watering, because it spreads spores. Spray with Bordeaux if the temperature is below 24°C. Try a soluble aspirin spray (make with one tablet to one cup of water); or dust foliage with powered sulphur. Compost-fed plants and those mulched with comfrey or lucerne are more resistant to rust. Regular seaweed, nettle or comfrey sprays may provide some resistance.

DWARF BEAN

BEAN FLIES

Symptoms: Plants or leaves collapse because of tunnelling in stems.
Solution: Spray with dilute clay spray, pikelet, marigold or garlic spray; try traps made with boards, painted yellow and covered in glue or motor oil; dust with derris every three days; shape soil in hills around the plant bases to encourage new roots, or mulch halfway up the stem with well-rotted hay, manure or compost. This will encourage new roots; vigorously growing plants are more resistant to bean fly.

Climbing beans are more resistant to bean fly and snake beans are relatively unaffected. In bad areas, try growing beans in cooler weather. Bean fly is usually related to poor soil. After two or three years of fertilising with compost, the problem should disappear. Plant masses of flowering umbelliferae such as fennel and parsnips, as well as grevilleas, and encourage predators to control the problem naturally.

CURLING BEANS

Beans curl in cool weather. They will straighten as it gets hotter.

FUNGUS DISEASES

Symptoms: Brown patches on leaves of beans; rotting stems; beans stuck together with brown–white fungus patches.

Solution: Spray with Bordeaux or baking soda spray if the temperature is below 24°C; treat every two days with chamomile, chive or milk sprays. Plants mulched with comfrey or compost are more resistant, and will grow new roots to increase nutrient uptake.

RED SPIDER MITES

Symptoms: Slight webbing on foliage, and dull, rough leaves.

Solution: A good overhead watering should control red spider mite problems. Interplant with marigolds, nasturtiums or mustard to repel them. Use milk, pikelet, anise or coriander sprays. Mulch halfway up the stem with well-rotted hay, manure or compost. This will encourage new roots; vigorously growing plants are more resistant to mites.

ROTTING SEED

Solution: Bean seed rots in cold, wet weather. For early plantings, coat seed with salad oil first. Add a sprinkle of white pepper to discourage ants, or dust with used powdered tea leaves.

BEETROOT

BOLTING

Symptoms: Beetroot go to seed before they have produced good roots.

Solution: Plants may have been sown in soil that is too cold, or sown too late in the season to mature before they go to seed in spring; the soil may be too rich in nitrogen, which produces leaf growth not root growth. Too much shade from tall plants such as corn or by overhanging trees may be the cause. Grow beetroots after a 'hungry' crop such as lettuce, or mulch with a low-nitrogen mulch such as shredded newspaper or sawdust.

BORON DEFICIENCY

Symptoms: Brown, sunken patches on the beetroot.

Solution: Use compost or good quality mulch; try a foliar spray from materials brought in from outside the area.

LEAF MINERS

Symptoms: White, skeletonised lines through the leaves.

Solution: Try tansy antifeedant spray or any of the repellent sprays; use bug juice; dust leaves with ground rock phosphate; try onion or garlic spray. Interplant crop with marigolds or surround it with a hedge of clipped wormwood or nasturtiums in pots.

LEAF SPOT FUNGUS

Symptoms: Pale to dark brown spots on the leaves.

Solution: Avoid overhead watering; mulch; spray with horsetail or chamomile tea; use Bordeaux in cold weather. In bad cases, use a horto paper, weed mat or newspaper mulch.

POWDERY MILDEW

Symptoms: Leaves have a white covering.

Solution: As above; use Bordeaux in cold weather; in hot, humid weather a dust of dolomite may help, but beware of increasing soil alkalinity; dust with powdered sulphur; use Condy's crystals spray. In bad cases, use a horto paper, weed mat or mulch of old newspaper.

BRASSICAS (BRUSSEL SPROUT, CAULIFLOWER, BROCCOLI, CABBAGE)

BLACK CABBAGE ROT

Symptoms: Leaves develop V-shaped brown patches that become thin and brittle. Affected seedlings often die.

Solution: Practise crop rotation; clear all infected material from old crops; cover ground with clear plastic for three weeks after an infection. Good compost inhibits black cabbage rot, especially if made with lucerne hay. Try a chive or double-strength garlic spray.

CABBAGE WHITE BUTTERFLIES,
CABBAGE MOTH CATERPILLARS

Symptoms: Skeletonised foliage; young plants may be eaten to the ground.

Solution: Surround the beds with strongly perfumed herbs such as lavender, or interplant with almost any other crop; the more interplanting, the smaller the problem will be. Cabbage moths and butterflies recognise their food supply by the scent and silhouette; disguise cabbages et al to protect the crop.

Always leave some brassicas from last season going to seed, or plant some especially for that purpose six months before planting your real crop. Adult butterflies will feed on the brassica blossom, then lay their eggs on the leaves below, ignoring the seedlings. Wild brassica weeds are also good trap crops.

Once the caterpillars are attacking the plants, try squashing them. The squashed, stationary caterpillars attract birds, wasps and other predators, which will then start eating the live ones, too. Encourage a good weed or bush community around the garden so that there are plenty of caterpillars around and the predators to eat them. This will eliminate the lag between pest and predator build-up.

Upended egg shells in the beds may sometimes outfox the butterflies. Strips or beds of white clover around or between the crop may also deter them.

Try tansy antifeedant or any of the repellent sprays. As a final resort, use pikelet spray; dust with white pepper; dust leaves with powdered rock phosphate; treat with dilute clay spray; try Dipel or derris; use bug juice, white pepper, garlic or wormwood sprays.

CLUBROOT

Symptoms: Roots are large and knobby; plants may wilt and die (especially in hot weather), or just grow slowly.

Solution: Protect the crop from nematodes with a companion crop of crotalaria or mustard. Maintain steady levels of decomposing organic matter, especially in sandy areas, where clubroot is worst.

Try nematode barriers using old tin cans with their tops and bottoms cut out as root guards. Add a sprinkle of lime or dolomite to the soil to reduce acidity. Practise stringent crop rotation for at least four years before any of the cabbage family, or swedes or turnips, are grown in that spot again.

LOOSE BROCCOLI HEADS

Solution: Pick sooner.

MAGNESIUM DEFICIENCY

Symptoms: The most obvious symptom of this common problem is brittle areas between the veins.

Solution: Give each plant one teaspoon of dolomite, well watered in. Try foliar sprays for large plants.

MOLYBDENUM DEFICIENCY

Symptoms: This mostly affects cauliflowers, but other brassicas can also suffer. Plants are stunted, yellow, with thin or distorted leaves and may not produce good sprouts or centres.

Solution: Most Australian soils are at least slightly molybdenum deficient. Compost made from material which is molybedenum deficient will also be deficient.

The traditional cure is molybdate dissolved in hot water and used as a foliage spray rich in molybdenum. Make a molybdenum spray by soaking comfrey or cauliflower leaves (from a different area) in water until the water turns pale green. Spray morning and dusk for three days then weekly.

SLUGS

Put a sharp collar made from an old tin can lid (or a ring of crinkled aluminium foil) around each cabbage stalk. Drizzle derris spray through the leaves, so it penetrates as much as possible, but wash vegetables very well before eating, as the derris may still be present. See Slugs and snails, p. 48–49.

SUN-SCORCHED CAULIFLOWERS

Symptoms: Yellow or purple cauliflower heads.
Solution: These have been exposed to too much direct sunlight. Curl the leaves over while they are maturing.

PHOSPHOROUS DEFICIENCY

Symptoms: Cabbages are pale and do not last.
Solution: Apply ground rock phosphate or old hen manure.

POTASH DEFICIENCY

Symptoms: Brittle areas on leaf edges.
Solution: Sprinkle wood ash and water well; for a short-term solution, try a foliar spray.

CARROT

BACTERIAL SOFT ROT

Symptons: Carrots rot and smell.
Solution: Soft rot is usually a post-harvest problem, when damaged carrots are stored in plastic or badly ventilated areas. If it occurs in the ground, the carrots have probably been damaged by weeding or digging. Mulch instead of weeding, or water first and pull instead of digging. (See Weeds, Chapter 3.) Make sure soil is well drained. Do not replant carrots for at least three years in areas where rot has been a problem.

To prevent soft rot in storage, dry carrots in the sun after pulling. Keep in a well-ventilated spot. Use netting or paper bags, not plastic bags.

CARROT APHIDS

Symptoms: Small green insects congregate on the underside of the carrot tops.
Solution: Try a vigorous hosing. As a last resort, use marigold or pyrethrum spray. Grow marigolds or nasturtiums between and around carrots to deter aphids; a nearby hedge of clipped wormwood will help.

CARROT FLY LARVAE

Solution: Larvae burrow into the roots. As they prefer straight rows, sow carrots in blocks instead. For bad cases, sow carrot seed with spring onion seed or keep a permanent band of spring onions round the bed. The onions must be actively growing, and there must be at least as many onions as carrots.

CRACKED CARROTS

Solution: Carrots crack with uneven watering or too much rain. Plant in a well-drained spot, and mulch. Alternating very wet and very dry soil is a sure recipe for cracking.

FORKED CARROTS

Solution: Carrots may have been forced to fork by stones in the soil, although well-fertilised carrots in compost-rich soil, even if the soil below is rock-hard, tend to grow up and straight if they cannot grow down. Add compost or good mulch. Carrots also fork when the soil is over-rich in nitrogen; grow after a greedy crop such as lettuce or brassica.

NEMATODES, ROOT EELWORMS

Symptoms: Deformed, lumpy carrots with small swellings on the top.
Solution: Try a preliminary crop of mustard. Keep up levels of organic matter. Mulch. Compost will inhibit nematodes; the best control is a good layer of steadily decomposing mulch, with a scatter of high-nitrogen material such as old hen manure or urine. As a temporary measure, use 1 part molasses in 9 parts water to dehydrate

nematodes. In bad cases leave ground fallow for a month, without any cover, including weeds. A rigorous crop rotation will keep nematode numbers down to non-pest levels.

PINK ROT
Solution: This is found in wet, badly drained soils. Improve drainage or raise the beds. In wet conditions, grow carrots with a no-dig method.

POOR GERMINATION
Solution: Carrots germinate poorly if the soil lacks humus and forms a thin crust on top. Sow carrot seed with radish seed; the radishes emerge first and break up the soil. Sprinkle a thin layer of lawn clippings or sawdust with carrot seed or cover the soil with hessian until seeds sprout. If ants are a problem, add some white pepper to the carrot seed.

BOLTING
Carrots may lack nitrogen or phosphorous; feed with mulch or compost. More probably they have been sown too late in autumn or too early in spring. While carrots survive most frosts, they will go to seed in any warm weather after a cold spell. Some varieties also tend to go to seed in very hot weather, or if grown in too much shade.

CAPSICUM

FAILURE TO RIPEN
Solution: Capsicums can be picked and eaten when they are green and tiny. In cold areas, pull up the whole plant before the first frost (which would rot the maturing fruit) and hang the plant up, soil and all. The capsicum will continue to mature for some weeks.

FRUIT FLIES
Symptons: Soft blisters on fruit.
Solution: See Fruit fly, p. 53–56.

FUNGUS SPOT
Symptoms: Brown spots on fruit and leaves.
Solution: Avoid overhead watering, especially in the late afternoon; spray with chamomile or horsetail tea, compost water or half-strength Bordeaux if the temperature is below 24°C. Do not spray flowers or fruit. Regular seaweed, nettle, comfrey or compost sprays may give some resistance. In very bad cases, use mulch, or horto paper, newspaper or a weed mat, to stop spores splashing up. A lucerne and comfrey mulch may also help.

CELERY

APHIDS
Symptoms: Twisted leaves.
Solution: See Chinese cabbage, p. 84.

CELERY LEAF SPOT
Symptoms: Dark spots and curling edges on the leaves.
Solution: Tear off affected stalks. Spray with chamomile tea every two days or Bordeaux every two weeks. Wash well before eating. A good mulch will reduce the problem, especially if made from compost, well-rotted lucerne hay, or half wattle bark and half wattle leaves, or a mixture of all of them, with some added hen manure to help break it down. Actively growing celery is more resistant to leaf spot; compost-grown celery is almost immune. Weekly seaweed, nettle or compost sprays will give a good deal of resistance. See Silverbeet, pp. 90–91.

DAMPING OFF
Symptoms: Seedlings die suddenly, often with a brown ring cut through at ground level.
Solution: See Seedlings, pp. 94–96.

SLUGS AND SNAILS
These love young celery. See Slugs and snails, pp. 48–49.

SMALL, TOUGH CELERY
Solution: Give more food and water. A weekly liquid manure should make the plants more succulent. Celery also toughens in spring as it goes to seed. Choose a modern cultivar.

CHICORY

BITTER CHICORY
Solution: Strongly growing, well-watered plants are less likely to be bitter. Cover the plants with an old box or flower pot for a week before picking, or blanch bitter leaves in boiling water before eating, to remove the sharpness.

CHINESE CABBAGE

APHIDS
Symptoms: Small insects on wilted or malformed leaves.
Solution: Wait at least three weeks if possible for predators; try strong jets of water, especially under the leaves; any of the repellent sprays such as tansy spray should be effective; try pikelet, dilute clay, seaweed or nettle sprays; grow marigolds as a companion crop; spray with marigold or nettle spray; derris, lantana, rhubarb, onion and elder sprays also kill aphids. Use a reflective aluminium foil mulch. As soil improves the aphid problem will lessen.

CATERPILLARS
Solution: See Brassicas, pp. 80–83.

RUNNING TO SEED WITHOUT HEARTING
Solution: The cabbages are probably maturing when the weather is warming up. Sow earlier in spring; mulch well as the soil warms up to insulate the plants.

SLUGS AND SNAILS
See Slugs and snails, pp. 48–49.

CHOKO

FAILURE TO MATURE
This is due to cool weather. Tiny chokoes are, however, good to eat.

ROOT ROTS
Solution: Plant in well-drained soil. Roots may also rot after frost damage. Strongly growing, well-fed plants cope with frost better. See Frost, pp. 21–23.

CUCUMBER

BITTER CUCUMBERS
These may be over-mature, left on the vines until their skins start to yellow. Cool weather followed by a hot spell can cause bitter cucumbers.
Solution: Pick earlier, or leave cucumbers to produce seeds for next year.

MELON APHIDS
Symptoms: These cluster in dense colonies under the leaves, which become stunted and curled as their sap is sucked. The winged females fly from plant to plant and populations build up rapidly in hot weather.
Solution: Try hosing the undersides of the leaves. See Chinese cabbage, above.

MILDEW
Symptoms: Powdery mildew leaves a grey film over the leaves; downy mildew makes foliage shrivel and leaves white clumps of fungus underneath.
Solution: See Zucchini, p. 94.

MISSHAPEN FRUIT
Solution: As this may be due to poor pollination, grow lemon balm or borage or other flowers around the garden or among the vegetables to attract bees.

NEMATODES
Symptoms: Young plants die.

Solution: Try a nematode guard; place a tin can with its top and bottom cut out around each seedling. See Carrot, pp. 82–83.

RED SPIDER MITES
Symptoms: Dull, rough foliage, sometimes a slight skeletonised look.
Solution: See Apple, p. 59.

EGGPLANT (AUBERGINE)

APHIDS
See Chinese cabbage, p. 84.

FAILURE TO MATURE
See Capsicum, p. 83.

MILDEW
Symptoms: Powdery film on leaves.
Solution: See Zucchini, p. 94.

SUNSCORCH
Symptoms: Blister-like, or pale or brownish patches on one side.
Solution: Grow eggplants in the shelter of taller plants such as corn or trellised cucumbers, or in a close-planted clump.

ENDIVE

SLUGS AND SNAILS
See Slugs and snails, pp. 48–49. Endive is a favourite slug and snail food.

GARLIC

COLLAR ROT
Solution: Keep fresh organic matter away from the stem in hot or humid weather. See also Root rots, pp. 56–57.

MILDEW
See Zucchini, p. 94.

ROOT ROT
Solution: Ensure soil is well drained and organic matter in the soil is decomposed before planting. If there is a recurrent problem, dress the soil with a compost made of 1 part wattle bark, 1 part wattle leaves, 4 parts lucerne hay and 1 part hen manure. To this, add up to 2 parts of a mixture of any of the following: comfrey leaves, chives, yarrow, chamomile flowers, horseradish leaves or nettle leaves.

SMALL BULBS OR CLOVES
Solution: Elephant garlic (really closer to a leek) has larger, milder cloves than true garlic. Plants grown in phosphorous- or nitrogen-deficient soils will also be smaller. The main cause of small bulbs is planting the cloves at the wrong time. It is best to plant in early autumn when the soil is still warm but cooling; the garlic will mature as the days shorten, then lengthen again. In warm areas, chill garlic for a month in the refrigerator before planting. New garlic cultivars may not need chilling. Their germination is not dependent on day-length.

LEEK

DOWNY MILDEW
Symptoms: Shrivelled leaf tips.
Solution: Once plants are badly affected, dig them out (they can be eaten). Do not replant leeks in an infected area for at least three years, and dispose of affected parts in a hot compost heap, or feed them to the hens.

LETTUCE

APHIDS
See Chinese cabbage, p. 84.

BIG–VEINED LETTUCE
Solution: This is a virus. Dig plants out and burn them. Only use seed from healthy plants. Practise crop rotation.

BITTER LETTUCE

Solution: Lettuces that have had any check in their growth may become bitter. Keep them well-watered and well-fed. Mulch heavily in hot weather. Lettuce going to seed may also be bitter.

BOLTING

Lettuce seedlings may appear to transplant well but run to seed prematurely.

Solution: If seedlings are large, cut off two-thirds of their tops when you plant them. This will reduce transpiration. In hot weather sprinkle them with water during the heat of the day for a few days and mulch well. Use bolt-resistant varieties such as Great Lakes, Narromar and red mignonette.

DOWNY MILDEW

Symptoms: Pale to dark brown spots on leaves.

Solution: Avoid overhead watering; mulch to stop splashing spores; spray with seaweed spray as a preventive; use half-strength Bordeaux, milk spray or chive or chamomile tea as controls to stop the problem spreading. Badly infected plants should be pulled out.

NON-HEARTING LETTUCE

This may be because of too much nitrogen and water at the expense of other necessary elements, especially during hot weather.

Solution: Avoid artificial nitrogen-rich fertilisers. Mulch well.

SLIMY LETTUCE

This is caused by too much overhead watering.

Solution: Mulch to keep soil moist and prevent contact between the lettuce and the soil, so that soil pathogens are not washed up onto the leaves during watering.

SLUGS AND SNAILS

See Slugs and snails, pp. 48–49.

MARROW

See Zucchini, p. 94.

MELON

MILDEW

Symptoms: Powdery mildew leaves a grey film over foliage; downy mildew means tufts of white fungus on the underside and shrivelled leaves with possible yellow splotches on the top.

Solution: Grow melons on a thick straw mulch, or on a trellis, or cascading out of old pipes, or stake them up slightly. Avoid overhead watering. Try growing them in a spadeful of compost on mown grass. Once melons are established, let animals such as chooks, wombats, wallabies, rabbits, sheep, etc. graze the grass. Even though the humidity is higher in grass than on soil, the plants seem healthier; perhaps spores find it harder to survive in the grass. See Lettuce, p. 85 and Zucchini, p. 94.

MUSHROOM

MUSHROOM FLIES

Symptoms: Tiny flies over mushrooms; maggots in vegetable.

Solution: Spray with pyrethrum spray; pick out infected mushrooms and old stalks every day.

OKRA

WOODY OKRA

Solution: Woody okra is too old; pick more frequently.

POOR GERMINATION

Solution: Soak seed for 24 hours in warm water, plant 1 cm deep, and wait two weeks.

CATERPILLARS
See Brassicas, pp. 80–83.

FUSARIUM AND VERTICULUM WILTS
See Tomato, pp. 92–93.

ONION

DOWNY MILDEW
Symptoms: Shrivelled tops.
Solution: See Lettuce, pp. 85–86.

NECK ROT
Symptoms: Squelchy, sulphur-smelling rotten onions.
Solution: Neck rot enters the onion through a wound. Ensure the tops have completely withered before they are cut off. Do not use spades or forks near onions; mulch them instead. Bordeaux, sprayed for mildew, tends to harden the outer layers of the onion and make it less susceptible to rotting. High-nitrogen fertilisers mean soft, susceptible growth.

ONION MAGGOTS
Symptoms: 5 mm light brown, hairy flies produce 7 mm long maggots that hollow out stems.
Solution: Wood ash between the plants will deter the flies, as will a barrier of aromatic herbs; build up sandy soil with mulch, but never dig decomposed organic matter into the soil.

THRIPS
Symptoms: White flecks on foliage; distorted leaves.
Solution: Grow with flowering companion plants such as pansies, poppies or white alyssum. These are excellent thrip lures and keep down weeds. See Apple, pp. 59–60.

WHITE ROT
Symptoms: Rotten onions covered in white fungus.
Solution: Ensure no undecomposed organic matter is dug into the soil; improve drainage.

PARSNIP

CANKER
Symptoms: Rotting, blackened parsnips.
Solution: Parsnips need good drainage. Leave all organic matter on top of the soil to decompose.

CARROT FLIES
See Carrot, pp. 82–83.

POOR GERMINATION
Solution: Parsnip seed is only viable for a year. Either collect seed or let the parsnips sow themselves naturally. Try soaking bought seed overnight then covering it with sacking until it germinates.

POWDERY MILDEW
Symptoms: Grey film on foliage.
Solution: See Zucchini, p. 94.

TOUGH PARSNIPS
These have been grown in poor soil or without enough moisture.
Solution: Mulch and apply slashed green manure crops.

PEA

BACTERIAL BLIGHT
Symptoms: Dark brown edges or splodges on leaves; stem may also develop splodges; both leaves and stem may shrivel.
Solution: Do not replant peas for at least three years in an affected area; use only healthy seed; collect all infected matter from a crop and burn or hot compost; do not pick or weed peas in wet weather; see Powdery mildew, below. Compost-fed plants are much more resistant, as are plants well mulched with rotting lucerne or wilted comfrey.

BIRDS
See Birds, p. 44.

EMPTY PODS
Solution: This may be frost damage. Wait for warmer weather.

LEAF SPOT
Symptoms: Dark spots on leaves.
Solution: See Powdery mildew, below.

POWDERY MILDEW
Symptoms: Powdery covering on foliage.
Solution: Stake the peas so air can flow around them. In humid areas angle the rows so that wind flows down them, not across, maximising the area exposed. See Zucchini, p. 94.

POTATO

APHIDS
Symptoms: Plants may wilt at the tips and die off. Large infestations can lead to premature dying off and reduced yield.
Solution: See Chinese cabbage, p. 84.

EELWORM NEMATODES
Symptoms: Wart-like swellings on potato skins.
Solution: Eelworm eggs and their larvae can survive two years in the soil. Plant an eelworm-resistant green manure crop such as rye, wheat or oats, or crops such as sweet corn, onions, cauliflowers and cabbage, all of which can tolerate eelworm.

Mulch to encourage earthworms. They eat eelworm eggs and larvae. Several species of fungi, encouraged by high levels of decomposing organic matter, trap eelworm in mycelium webs.

POTATO BLIGHT
Symptoms: The leaves have dark brownish spots which increase in size with a greenish white mould. Leaves die and lesions appear on the stems. Fungus spores are washed from the leaves to the tubers, which then rot. Potato blight can be carried by wind, water or infected plants.

Solution: Spray with Bordeaux in the early stages to prevent spores washing to the ground. Spray again after two weeks if symptoms continue. If symptoms appear near harvest, slash off the plant tops and burn or compost them. Then spray the stalks with Bordeaux.

POTATO CATERPILLARS
Symptoms: Caterpillars in rolled edges of leaves.
Solution: See Brassicas, pp. 80–83.

POTATO GANGRENE
Symptoms: Potatoes rot from inside, with deep, rounded depressions on the outside. The smell is horrible, like rotten fish.
Solution: Plant only disease-free seed. Try not to damage potatoes when digging up or weeding; potato gangrene only affects injured plants at harvest. Never store potatoes that are injured in any way, as injury can let fungus spores enter. Keep storage areas free of dirt and debris from past crops. Compost or actively rotting mulch may inhibit gangrene spores.

GREEN POTATOES
Solution: These have been exposed to sunlight. They are bitter and poisonous from an alkaloidal glucoside called solanine. Newly dug potatoes are most susceptible. Do not leave them on top of the ground before bagging. Store potatoes in a dark place.

Do not eat green potatoes. The greening indicates that the whole tuber has gone into growth mode, which is dangerous. Symptoms of solanine poisoning resemble those of gastroenteritis.

POTATO MOSAIC, LEAF ROLL
Symptoms: These are viral diseases carried by aphids from infected plants. The symptoms of both include rolled leaf edges. Plants may die early, with yellow veins in the leaves and (possibly) mottled spots.
Solution: These viruses cannot be cured once the plant is infected. Plant disease-free

tubers. Do not use small tubers with long thin shoots for seed potatoes as they may be infected with leaf roll.

The viruses will not remain in the soil after the tubers and aphids have gone. Crops can be planted in the same soil as long as no small potatoes remain (which is difficult to ensure).

POTATO MOTHS
Symptoms: Burrows in potatoes, which may then rot.
Solution: Make sure no tubers are exposed or the female moths can lay eggs in the potatoes. Hill soil around the plants and mulch regularly. Plant a companion crop of broad beans just before the potatoes, then slash it for mulch as the potatoes mature.

POTATO SCAB
Symptoms: Small, brown, circular or oval scabby encrustations on the potato. Potatoes may be affected under the soil with no sign above.
Solution: Plant disease-free tubers. Make sure drainage is good. Scab is most prevalent in wet soils with temperatures below 18°C. Spores can remain active in the soil for 15 years or more. To help inhibit scab, plant a crop of broad beans, then dig them in and leave them to rot before planting the potatoes. Compost-fed potatoes are far more resistant to scab.

COMMON SCAB
Symptoms: The scabs gradually cover the entire tuber. No symptoms may appear above ground.
Solution: Plant only certified (clean) seed. Common scab is introduced on infected tubers. It can also infect beetroot and turnips; these should not be grown anywhere where next season's potatoes will be planted.

Common scab is worse in dry, warm conditions and light, sandy soils. Mulch well. Make sure soil is kept moist around potatoes, particularly when the tubers are forming.

Avoid liming potato beds. Once scab is present, spread green manure on the soil before planting and add plenty of compost. Compost, and most decomposing organic matter, will probably encourage soil microorganisms antagonistic to scab.

RHIZOCTONIA SCAB
Symptoms: New shoots rot, foliage is bunched or curled, potatoes have cracks or depressions with brownish black scabby lumps on them.
Solution: Rhizoctonia scab is worst in cool wet weather. Ensure soil is well mulched and drained and that seed is disease free, with no blemishes. Feed.

SOGGY POTATOES
Solution: These are lacking in potash. Add wood ash to the soil (not too much or the soil may become too alkaline). Mulch with comfrey or good compost. Old potatoes are also softer.

TARGET SPOT
Symptoms: This is later, more widespread and slower-acting than potato blight. Small spots appear on the leaves, which eventually die off. This happens so slowly that the grower may think the plants are dying off naturally. Yield will be much reduced.
Solution: Spray with Bordeaux when symptoms appear and every two weeks from then on.

PUMPKIN

APHIDS
Symptoms: Twisted leaves.
Solution: Pumpkins are usually growing so strongly that aphids do not matter. Squash between your fingers on new shoots.

MILDEWS
Solution: Limit overhead watering. Water in

the morning so the leaves are not wet overnight. Stake the vine to let air circulate around the leaves. Grow on top of mulch to avoid soil contact. See Zucchini, p. 94.

THRIPS

Symptoms: Small insects in flowers.
Solution: Keep pumpkins growing strongly and thrips will not be a problem. See Apple, pp. 59–60.

RADISH

CRACKED RADISHES

Solution: Avoid extremes of wet and dry. Mulch.

HOT RADISHES

Solution: Pick the radishes when they are younger.

TWISTED RADISHES

These have been grown in hard, dry or grass-infested soil, and so have colonised the air instead of the ground.
Solution: Improve the living standards of the next radish crop and they will stay earthbound.

RHUBARB

BACTERIAL CROWN ROT

Symptoms: Crown rots; young leaves shrivel.
Solution: Dig out affected plants; burn them or put them in hot compost. Leave the holes where the plants were open to sunlight for three weeks or spray with Bordeaux. Spray the remaining crop with Bordeaux in winter; Treat plants with chamomile tea or elder spray in summer.

BEETLES

Solution: Surround with a companion crop of chrysanthemums; dust with talcum powder or diatomaceous earth; use pikelet spray. A derris spray can be used as a last resort (spray the leaves, not the beetles).

DOWNY MILDEW, RUST AND LEAF SPOT

Solution: Do not overwater. Make sure soil is well drained. Do not overfertilise, especially in winter. See Lettuce, pp. 85–86.

GREEN RHUBARB

This is not a problem; there are green varieties which will not turn red as they ripen.

TOO MANY LEAVES

Solution: The rhubarb has been given too much nitrogen at the expense of other nutrients. A good quality mulch or compost will suffice.

SHALLOT

WHITE ROTS AND DOWNY MILDEW

Solution: Make sure all organic matter in the soil is well rotted; do not dig it in until decomposed or do not dig at all.

SILVERBEET

FUNGUS LEAF SPOT

Symptoms: Brown spots on leaves.
Solution: Keep plants growing strongly. In trials here with three lots of silverbeet side by side, the patch fed with compost did not get leaf spot, while the artificially fed patch did. The patch fed with pelletised hen manure did get leaf spot, but not as much as the artificially fed patch.

As a temporary control, pick off affected leaves. They can be eaten, or composted if they are really grotty. Spray the rest with chamomile tea every week, preferably mixed with seaweed or nettle spray. If this fails, try elder spray, double-strength garlic spray, Bordeaux or baking soda sprays in the cool of the evening. These sprays may burn the leaves but will destroy the fungus so that new leaves are unblemished. Try the other remedies first, and remember that a slight case of spot does no harm to the plant.

PALE, STUNTED SILVERBEET
Solution: Feed with high-nitrogen fertilisers such as blood and bone, liquid manure, old hen manure, good mulch or diluted urine.

SPINACH

BOLTING
Solution: Grow only in cool weather; plant bolt-resistant varieties such as Slow Bolt and Summertime. Mulch well and renew the mulch as the weather warms up in spring, to keep the soil cool longer and increase the harvest.

SQUASH

See Zucchini, p. 94 and Pumpkin, pp. 89–90.

SUNFLOWER

PARSNIP CANKER
Symptoms: General decline, root rot, spotted leaves.
Solution: Remove all affected plants and burn. Improve soil drainage. Do not plant sunflowers or parsnips there for at least three years.

SWEDE

APHIDS
Symptoms: Small clusters of insects on foliage, twisted leaves.
Solution: Spray with soapy water or pikelet spray. If this fails, use marigold, garlic or pyrethrum sprays; keep plants growing strongly and they should outgrow the pests. Do not add a high-nitrogen fertiliser to swedes (this will encourage pests); simply grow them in ground that has been well-manured for the previous crop. As soil improves, the problem should disappear.

CATERPILLARS
Solution: See Brassicas, pp. 80–83.

ROOT ROTS
Solution: Plant only in well-drained soil; make sure all organic matter in the soil is decomposed, or leave it on top to subside naturally. Pull out all affected plants at once and leave the holes open to the sun. Soak the soil around each plant with a double-strength garlic spray.

SWEET CORN

CATERPILLARS, CORN EAR WORMS
Symptoms: These heliothis caterpillars burrow into the corn ears and eat the kernels. They can be difficult to get at and the tough covering of the ear protects them from predators, dusts and sprays.
Solution: Check corn ears for droppings and sawdust-like deposits. Remove the outer coverings, squash the pest, then smooth everything back into place. Injections of oil spray behind the covering may be effective but squashing is better, and less work. Alternatively, to deter caterpillars, wipe the silk with mineral oil once a week or apply derris dust. Try a tansy antifeedant spray in the early morning so the silk has a chance to dry out by midmorning. (If it stays wet and claggy, poor pollination may result.)

The best prevention is a high bird and predator population. Plant flowering parsnips or other flowering umbelliferae around the crop to attract wasps, hoverflies, spiders and other predators.

EELWORMS, CUTWORMS, NEMATODES

Symptoms: Young plants die, apparently cut at the ground.

Solution: The best long-term cure is compost or any mulch that will rapidly decompose. Add a scatter of pelletised hen manure or other high-nitrogen material on top of the mulch to encourage it to break down. Maintain high levels of organic matter, especially in sandy soil.

As a short-term measure, stake each seedling with two toothpicks so that it cannot be cut, or place each seedling in its own miniature greenhouse made out of the top of an old plastic bottle. (This will also speed up growth.) Drizzle a solution of 1 part molasses to 19 parts water around the plants. Plant a green manure mustard crop (which takes only six to eight weeks) before sowing large crops of corn in sandy areas. Help the green manure to break down with a scatter of hen manure or even sulphate of ammonia. See Seedlings, pp. 94–96.

HARD CORN

Solution: This is produced by maize, not sweet corn. Maize is only tender when very young. Occasionally sweet corn seed is mixed with maize seed, or has been collected from maize plants accidentally (sometimes because their parent has been cross-pollinated by maize, or some other genetic accident has occurred). Feed hard corn to the hens, grind it for polenta or add it to slow cooking stews.

POOR POLLINATION

Solution: Corn should be planted in blocks at least one metre wide, to help pollination. The male tassel on top of the corn stalk produces pollen which must be shed onto the silk below. If the corn is planted in one long row, place brown paper bags over some of the male tassels; shake the tassel well inside the bags to catch the pollen, then lightly shake the pollen onto the silks. Occasionally

male tassels finish producing their pollen before the silks are ready below. If this happens, try to find another crop of corn and borrow some pollen.

SWEET POTATO

CUTWORMS

Symptoms: Large areas of eaten foliage.

Solution: Drizzle a solution of 1 part molasses to 19 parts water on soil. Stake plants upwards out of reach; mulch with compost; keep up levels of organic matter in the soil, especially in sandy areas. Try mustard as a companion crop; plant two weeks before the sweet potatoes and keep slashing it to create an aromatic, fast-decomposing mulch around the sweet potato plants. This may have a limited effect the first year, but by the second it should be an excellent control. See Seedlings, pp. 94–96.

TOMATO

BIRDS

See Birds, p. 44.

BLOSSOM END ROT

Symptoms: Dark patches on the fruit.

Solution: Blossom end rot is due to irregular watering or lack of calcium. Mulch well to reduce water stress. A calcium foliar spray will increase calcium; a seaweed, compost, nettle or other 'green' spray every few days will also help. A half-strength Bordeaux spray can also be used, but as Bordeaux will kill predators as well as help the blossom rot, try to cure the calcium deficiency first. If the soil is calcium-deficient, add dolomite to the garden generally, or bring in materials for mulch and compost from other areas.

BLOTCHY TOMATOES

Solution: Hard yellow patches on ripe or

A tomato plant with root knot caused by nematode damage. A deep decomposing mulch over the plant will encourage earthworms, mycelium webs and other soil organisms that control root knot.

Bulbs may be damaged by a number of pests and diseases. Store them carefully in cool, dry conditions and plant only fat, firm bulbs.

Often regarded as a nuisance, lichens in fact help trees to resist pests and diseases and should not be removed.

Let a range of vegetables go to seed throughout the year in order to attract predators to your garden.

near-ripe tomatoes are usually caused by phosphorous or potash deficiency. Try a foliar tea made with potash or phosphorous-rich materials: compost, seaweed, hen manure, comfrey, urine.

CABBAGE WHITE BUTTERFLY CATERPILLARS
See Brassicas, pp. 80–83.

CRACKED TOMATOES
Solution: These are a result of fluctuating moisture levels. Thick mulch and well-drained soil will help prevent the problem. Don't let tomatoes dry out between waterings; don't saturate them, either. Keep plenty of organic matter in the soil with frequently renewed mulch to help regulate moisture levels.

CUTWORMS
Symptoms: Plants appear suddenly cut off at the base.
Solution: See Seedlings, pp. 94–96.

DAMPING OFF
Symptoms: Seedlings suddenly die; watch for a brownish band at ground level.
Solution: Dip seedlings in chamomile tea before planting; pour the rest around each one on planting. Make sure all organic matter in the soil is decomposed and no mulch is actually touching the seedlings.

FRUIT FLIES
Symptoms: Maggots in fruit.
Solution: Use traps and repellents. Pick fruit regularly. Do not let fallen fruit lie on the ground. As a last resort, pick green tomatoes and let them ripen indoors or cover them with a fruit fly-proof net made of old pantyhose with a wire support. See Fruit fly, pp. 53–56.

FUSARIUM WILT
Symptoms: Plant wilts, rotted at the base of the stem; stems may be cracked; in mild cases the plant may be stunted or grow slowly.

Solution: This is a soil-borne fungus. Before planting, try covering the soil with clear plastic sheeting for three weeks to kill off spores in the soil. Practise crop rotation; use resistant cultivars.

As soon as symptoms appear, try double-strength garlic spray on stems, soil and foliage. Seedlings can be dipped in garlic spray before planting out, with a little drizzled onto nearby soil. Soils high in potash are more resistant to fusarium wilt. Try adding wood ash or compost. In bad cases dig out plants and burn them. The spores are both wind- and soil-borne and will easily spread to neighbouring plants. Cover the hole with clear plastic and drench the soil in double-strength garlic spray.

POOR FRUIT SET
Solution: This may mean too much nitrogen, particularly if foliage is thick and green; use mulch, compost, etc. (see Fertility, pp. 15–17). Try adding ground rock phosphate as a temporary measure. Some tomato varieties do not set well in cool weather; cold climate varieties may not set in very hot weather.

RED SPIDER MITES
Symptoms: Webbed leaves.
Solution: A good overhead watering every day may be all that is needed. In bad cases, use any of the repellent sprays or, as a last resort, spray tops and undersides of the leaves with white oil in temperatures below 24°C, or with soap or pyrethrum spray in the evenings.

SLUGS AND SNAILS
See Slugs and snails, pp. 48–49.

TURNIP

APHIDS
Symptoms: Clusters of small, whitish insects on the leaves.
Solution: Keep turnips growing strongly. If the problem persists, try tansy spray, any of the

other repellent sprays or pikelet spray. Aphids should not warrant poisons.

CATERPILLARS
Solution: See Brassicas,' pp. 80–83.

WOODY TURNIPS
Solution: Pick them younger; add compost to the soil so the next crop will develop succulent roots.

ZUCCHINI

POWDERY MILDEW
Symptoms: A powdery deposit over the leaves; these may yellow and die.
Solution: Do not grow these in hot, humid weather if possible. Keep foliage dry by avoiding overhead watering or watering early in the morning. Mulch well to stop spores splashing up onto the plant. In cool conditions zucchini may be sprayed with Bordeaux or Condy's crystals but leaves will burn if the temperature is above 24°C. (Young leaves may be burnt at any time.) Spray soapy water in the cool of the evenings, avoiding flowers. Spray chamomile tea or elder spray at any time. Pick out infected leaves as soon as they appear and burn them or hot compost them.

Young and vigorously growing zucchini are more resistant to powdery mildew. If mildew has been a problem before, plant a second zucchini crop a couple of months after the first, in a well-drained, airy spot away from the first crop, in case it is infected. Zucchini grown at the edge of raised beds will trail out over the grass; grass-grown zucchini seem more resistant to powdery mildew than those grown on bare soil in the garden. I also plant some in high concrete pipes and unused clay sewage pipes; zucchinis trail down the pipes, ripen early, and are relatively immune from powdery mildew. Zucchini are sometimes scarred by sunburn in very hot weather.

SEEDLINGS

FAILURE TO EMERGE FROM THE SOIL:
• Ants may eat the seed. Before sowing, cover seed with a mixture of oil and white pepper or sow with dried tea leaves or a little talcum powder. See also Ants, p. 7.

• Seeds can rot in cold weather. Wait until it is warmer, or sow them in pots indoors and transplant or, if sowing outside, first cover them in a little oil.

• Failure to germinate is usually because seed was too old or stored badly. This may not be the packager's fault; seed is sometimes kept far too hot or cold or for too long, especially if it is not bought from a garden centre. Some seeds, such as parsnip and angelica, are viable for only a very short time. Save your own where possible.

• Baked or crusty soil can prevent seedlings emerging. Scatter a very light layer of dried grass clippings (the seedlings will not be able to penetrate too thick a layer), almost enough to cover the soil. This will retain a little moisture. When the seedlings are about a finger high, start mulching. In very hard soil consider sowing crop seed with the seed of miniature radishes. These will push their way through almost anything, carving a way for the less vigorous seedlings to follow. Either pull out the radish seedlings or wait a few months and pick the crop. Cover the ground with mosquito netting to help keep in some moisture so that the surface layer does not get too hard.

• Weed competition can stop seedlings emerging or smother them when they do.

• Some plants, such as brassicas, produce natural herbicides, especially when they are going to seed, that inhibit seed germination. A previous brassica or sunflower crop may mean that seeds planted in the same place may take longer to germinate, or may not germinate at all. Commercial herbicides, of course, can have the same effect.

FAILURE TO THRIVE:
• Starvation. Feed them with a soluble fertiliser such as hen manure or a mixture of 1 part urine to 20 parts water, then add compost or good mulch.

• Thirst. Water; mulch to reduce watering needs, or use miniature greenhouses made of cut-off soft drink bottles to conserve water. Don't use these in very hot weather unless the bottles are made of slightly tinted glass.

• Cold. Cover plants with miniature green-houses as above.

• Heat. Mulch the soil well and water from overhead to cool them down. Providing shade cloth over the top helps seedlings survive in very hot weather until their roots are well established.

WHY SEEDLINGS DISAPPEAR:
• Slugs and snails are the most common culprits, especially if the seedlings disappear overnight. See Slugs and snails, pp. 48–49.

• A sudden wilting or a brown rim at the base of the plant is usually caused by damping off. See below.

• Seedlings snapped off overnight may have been attacked by cutworm. See below.

• Birds, especially starlings, may pull out young seedlings. See Birds, p. 44. Rats can sometimes eat seedlings, particularly corn. So will wallabies, rabbits and, more rarely, wombats, kangaroos and bandicoots. See Rabbits, pp. 47–48.

• Extreme heat will kill seedlings.

• Severe frost will kill seedlings, sometimes withering them so severely that the remains are hard to find. See Frost, pp. 21–23.

DAMPING OFF
Symptoms: Seedlings may suddenly wilt and die, especially in wet conditions, humid weather or if there is a high level of undigested organic matter in the soil. There may be a narrow wilted or brownish collar near ground level.
Prevention: Don't plant seedlings directly into mulch, particularly in hot, humid areas. Part the mulch to leave a small space round each seedling and do not pull until the plant is growing strongly. Make sure all organic matter in the soil is well rotted before planting seedlings. Try leaving it on top instead of digging it in.
Control: Dip seedlings, soil and all, in chamomile tea before planting. Drizzle about half a cup of chamomile tea around each plant. Repeat this every two days for a couple of weeks. The seedlings should then be tough enough to withstand damping off.

CUTWORM
The main symptom of cutworm is a wilting plant that has been chewed off just above soil level.

Prevention:
• Mulch regularly, especially with good compost; this will help destroy breeding sites and encourage a parasitic fungus. Grow mustard and slash it for mulch. Leaf mulch is also said to repel cutworms.

• Interplant crops with herbs, onions and marigolds.

• With bad large-scale infestations, autumn or spring fallowing will help. Be scrupulous with weed control; the ground must be totally fallow.

• Never plant seedlings just after a crop of weeds has been dug in.

• Improve drainage if necessary; cutworms are often worst in badly drained soil or in sandy soil.

• Encourage predators: parasitic fungus (use frequently renewed mulch and added high-nitrogenous material such as manure or urine to break it down), flies and wasps, beetles, birds such as ibises, starlings, magpies, crows, yellow robins and kookaburras.

• Maintain a humus-rich soil. This is the most effective cutworm prevention.

Control:

• Try cutworm bait. Mix 1 part bran with 1 part hardwood sawdust, 2 parts of molasses and enough water to moisten. Spread this mixture around seedlings. It will attract the cutworms which become sticky and helpless, unable to burrow back into the soil. They will die of heat or starvation or be picked off by birds.

• Spray Dipel on seedling roots and around the soil when planting.

• Dig up affected seedlings at once.

• Stick toothpicks to the left and right of each seedling, as if splinting a broken leg.

• Place 'collars' of old cans or cardboard toilet rolls around the plant, pressed into the soil to fence off the roots.

• Before planting, place clear plastic sheets on the soil for three weeks during hot weather to kill cutworms.

CHAPTER EIGHT

ORNAMENTALS:

FLOWERS, PLANTS, TREES AND SHRUBS

BLOSSOM PROBLEMS

For individual spray recipes, refer to Chapter Four, Organic Remedies (or see index).

Balled flowers. This is a fungal or bacterial problem. See Roses, pp. 121–23. Prune all spent flowers, because their sweetness can aggravate the problem; so can the sweet sticky secretions of aphids, woolly aphids and other sap-suckers, or the sweet sap of overhanging wattles or other 'sappy' trees.

Buds fail to open. This is often due to fungal or bacterial problems. Spray with Bordeaux before flowering or when shrubs are dormant. Regular seaweed sprays may ease a long-term problem. Sometimes trace element deficiencies may prevent buds opening.

Failure to flower. The plant may be in the wrong place: too shady, too hot, too cold or too sunny. Failure to flower may mean that the roots have been disturbed; this is common with camellias that have been planted while flowering the previous season. In some species, too much high-nitrogen fertiliser promotes lots of leaf growth at the expense of the flowers. In other species lack of flowers is caused by lack of feeding.

Flowers fall prematurely. This is usually due to poor feeding; in particular, lack of nitrogen or phosphorous. Sudden hot or cold spells can also cause flowers to drop prematurely. Mulch well to insulate and feed the soil.

Nibbled flowers. Common culprits are slugs and snails. See Slugs and snails, pp. 48–49; also see Earwigs under Roses, p. 122. Wombats are also blossom nibblers; bower birds love blue flowers but will take any flower; currawongs will tear up daffodils, and starlings can turn into flower nibblers.

FLOWERS

AGERATUM

APHIDS

Symptoms: Small green insects on foliage, distorted leaves.

Solution: Grow with tansy or marigolds or lavender (preferably dwarf) nearby. A clipped hedge of wormwood will also repel aphids. Try a tansy antifeedant spray. Spray with diluted Marmite or Vegemite to help attract predators such as lacewings and hoverflies; encourage birds and ladybirds by planting flowering shrubs and avoiding pesticides. Strong hosing or running your fingers over the pests may solve the problem. See Avocado, p. 61.

ALYSSUM

STEM ROT

Symptoms: Drooping plant; stem rotted at ground level.

Solution: Remove infected plants and burn. Leave holes open to sun for three weeks. Remove dead foliage at the base of other plants to improve air circulation; water remaining plants and the soil around them with chamomile or chive tea. Make sure there is no undecomposed organic matter in the soil.

ASTER

POWDERY MILDEW

Symptoms: Powdery deposits on leaves.

Solution: Try a companion crop of chamomile around the plants. See Zucchini, p. 94.

ASTER GRUB

Symptoms: Centre leaves distorted together.

Solution: Cut off affected leaves. Spray with pikelet spray or dust with talcum powder or diatomaceous earth. Try a tansy antifeedant spray. If the pest persists, use Dipel or derris spray.

RED SPIDER MITES

Symptoms: Dull, pitted foliage.

Solution: These are worse if the plant is sheltered from the rain by overhanging trees or eaves. In bad cases, do not grow the flower there again.

Companion planting with marigolds (tagetes not calendula) may help. As soil improves, mites should only be a problem in rare, unseasonal years. See Apple, p. 59.

ASTILBE

BROWN LEAF MARGINS

Solution: This is caused by fluctuating soil moisture. Water thoroughly and regularly. The soil may have a potash deficiency, so add wood ash, comfrey mulch, or a good compost. Make compost with materials from outside your garden, as home-grown materials may also be potash-deficient.

BEDDING BEGONIA

BROWN VEGETABLE WEEVIL

Symptoms: Brown-edged leaves.

Solution: Spray with pyrethrum, and mulch well. Try a tansy antifeedant spray. In bad cases, as a temporary solution only, use a weed mat mulch.

BELLIS PERENNIS

RUST

Symptoms: Raised orange dots on leaves.

Solution: Spray plants with aspirin spray

(1 soluble tablet to 1 cup water); spray plants and soil with chamomile tea. Use Bordeaux in temperatures below 24°C. Mulch well. Companion plant with chives or chamomile.

CALENDULA

RUST

Symptoms: Large, rusty circles on leaves or stems.
Solution: See *Bellis Perennis*, p. 98.

CANTERBURY BELL

APHIDS

Symptoms: Aphids cluster on new shoots; older leaves curl under at the edges.
Solution: See Ageratum, p. 98.

POWDERY MILDEW

Symptoms: Powdery deposits on foliage.
Solution: See Zucchini, p. 94.

RED SPIDER MITES

Symptoms: Sand-blasted, dull leaves.
Solution: See Aster, p. 98.

CARNATION

FROST DAMAGE

Symptoms: Hollow buds.
Solution: See Frost, pp. 21–23.

MILDEW OR LEAF SPOT

Symptoms: Dark spots on leaves.
Solution: Try any of the fungicides suggested for mildew under Zucchini, p. 94.

RUST

Symptoms: Rusty spots on leaves.
Solution: In bad cases, use a weed mat mulch to lower humidity around the plants. Companion planting with chamomile is effective. See *Bellis Perennis*, pp. 98–99.

THRIPS

Symptoms: Streaked flowers.
Solution: Some thrips are useful predators because they eat mites and aphids. Do not destroy thrips unless they are badly damaging plants. Rain or overhead water will significantly reduce numbers. Encourage wasps, bugs, spiders, fungi, ladybirds, lacewings and other predators. A good watering is the best control.

Thrips are worse in gardens with winter-flowering weeds; their numbers increase, and when the weeds die off the thrips transfer to flowers. In the long term, plant more ground covers and spread mulch over winter-flowering weeds.

CHRYSANTHEMUM

BUD GRUB

Symptoms: Brown, sunken patches in flower buds.
Solution: Try a tansy antifeedant spray. In bad cases spray with pyrethrum, mixed with a little soapy water to aid penetration; mulch well and renew the mulch layer regularly (1 part comfrey to 2 parts strongly scented herbs such as wormwood, mustard, crotalaria or tansy).

LEAF EELWORM

Symptoms: Shrivelled, blackened foliage.
Solution: Try a tansy antifeedant spray. In bad cases saturate ground with a solution of 1 part molasses to 9 parts water. Increase humus levels by adding compost to inhibit the eelworm. In very bad cases use a weed mat, horto paper or old newspaper mulch around the plants. Continually replaced mulch or compost is the best long-term solution, particularly if the soil is sandy. Avoid mulches such as wood chips, which take a long time to break down.

MITES
Symptoms: Pale tracery on leaves.
Solution: Hose well (especially under the leaves) and check next day; the tracery on the leaves will still be there, but the pests may have gone. If the pests have gone, hose every day for a few weeks until predator numbers build up. Spray with oil spray if the temperature is below 20°C, with soapy water if it is below 24°C, or with pikelet, pyrethrum or dilute clay sprays. Companion planting with dwarf marigolds (tagetes not calendula) may help.

CINERARIA

LEAF MINER
Symptoms: Grey tracery on leaves.
Solution: See Chrysanthemum, p. 99.

DAHLIA

FAILURE TO FLOWER
Solution: This may be due to too much nitrogen, which causes lush foliage growth at the expense of flowers. Give a low-nitrogen mulch such as woodchips and a handful of ground rock phosphate. Dahlias are very responsive to soil temperature; they will flower in light semi-shade, but not at all in deep shade.

RED SPIDER MITES
Symptoms: Dull, pitted foliage.
Solution: See Aster, p. 98.

SLUGS AND SNAILS
Symptoms: Flowers and foliage eaten.
Solution: See Slugs and snails, pp. 48–49.

THRIPS
Symptoms: Tiny black insects and blackened edges to flowers.
Solution: See Carnation, p. 100.

DELPHINIUM

CROWN ROT
Symptoms: Plant wilts suddenly; stem rots at ground level.
Solution: Cut out affected plants; leave holes open to sunlight for three weeks; try to improve air flow by cutting out low growth. Spray unaffected plants and the soil around them with double-strength garlic and chamomile sprays. Companion planting with chamomile or thickly planted garlic may help.

MILDEW
Symptoms: Powdery deposit on foliage.
Solution: Interplant with chives, chamomile or garlic (which look lovely flowering with delphiniums). See Zucchini, p. 94.

FOXGLOVE

RED SPIDER MITES
Symptoms: Dull, brownish leaves.
Solution: See Aster, p. 98.

RUST
Symptoms: Red flecks on leaves.
Solution: The cultivar may be rust-prone. Plant a different variety or transplant the existing ones to a rust-free place. See *Bellis perennis*, pp. 98–99.

GERANIUM (PELARGONIUM)

BACTERIAL LEAF SPOT
Symptoms: Semi-transparent circles on leaves.
Solution: See Brown rot under Apricot, p. 60.

BOTRYTIS
Symptoms: Flowers rot in wet weather.
Solution: Cut off affected flowers, or any mature flower in wet weather; spray with chamomile tea, or Bordeaux when the

temperature is below 24°C. Companion planting with chamomile may help.

CATERPILLARS
Symptoms: Leaves or flowers eaten.
Solution: See Brassicas, pp. 80–83.

RUST
Symptoms: Yellow spots on tops of leaves; brown spots underneath.
Solution: See *Bellis perennis*, pp. 98–99.

STEM ROT
Symptoms: Sudden wilting; rotting stem at ground level.
Solution: Cut out affected part of plant and remove soil around it. Use the unaffected tips of plants as cuttings to propagate plant again. To sterilise the soil before planting, cook a shallow layer of soil on a tray in the oven with a medium-sized raw potato, until the potato is cooked. Any pathogens should by then be destroyed. Before planting geraniums in the garden, saturate the soil with double-strength garlic and chamomile sprays. Make sure there is no undecomposed organic matter in the soil near the plant and keep mulch away from the stem, especially in hot, humid weather.

GERBERA

APHIDS
Symptoms: Deformed flowers; deformed stems, sucked and twisted.
Solution: See Ageratum, p. 98. Interplant with any strongly scented herb (the silhouettes as well as the scents will confuse the aphids). Mulch will help control ants that may be bringing the aphids.

BUD GRUBS
Symptoms: Rotted centres in flowers.
Solution: Try a tansy antifeedant spray. Use Dipel, pyrethrum or white pepper sprays, mixed with a little soap to aid penetration.

CROWN ROT
Symptoms: Sudden wilting; rot at base.
Solution: Dig the clump out; wash off as much soil as possible; drench the whole plant, roots and all, with strong chamomile tea, garlic or Bordeaux spray. Replant it on soil slightly above the existing soil level, to improve drainage.

VIRUSES
Symptoms: Green flowers.
Solution: Control aphids which transmit viruses; cut out affected plants and burn. Do not replant the same flower there for least three years.

WHITE RUST
Symptoms: Raised white flecks on leaves and sometimes on stems.
Solution: See *Bellis perennis*, pp. 98–99.

HOLLYHOCK

RUST
Symptoms: Rusty spots on leaves.
Solution: Companion planting with garlic may help (at least six plants for each hollyhock). See *Bellis perennis*, pp. 98–99.

HOLES IN LEAVES
Solution: See Slugs and snails, pp. 48-49. Caterpillars may cause damage; use pikelet spray, white pepper, diatomaceous earth or Dipel.

RED SPIDER MITES
Symptoms: Dull, possibly yellowing foliage; mites are just visible to the naked eye.
Solution: See Aster, p. 98.

LAVENDER

MILDEW
Symptoms: Brown patches under foliage near ground.
Solution: Cut out affected foliage to improve

air circulation and light penetration; old plants should be replaced. In hot, humid places, dust plants with dolomite to help prevent attacks, and prune regularly.. In cold areas, prune in midsummer; mildew can follow frost damage and new growth is more frost resistant. Lavender should never be grown in shade or semi-shade as it needs at least three hours of direct sunlight each day, and good air flow.

FROST DAMAGE

Prune well in summer to encourage new growth. See Frost, pp. 21–23.

LOBELIA

JASSID LEAF HOPPERS

Symptoms: Dull cream mottling on foliage.
Solution: Try a tansy antifeedant spray. In bad cases try sprays of pyrethrum, derris, oil, double-strength garlic spray mixed with soap spray, or soapy water in cool weather.

MESEMBRYANTHEMUM

RUST

Symptoms: Yellow spots on leaves; leaves later shrivel.
Solution: Remove affected leaves as soon as you notice them. See *Bellis perennis*, pp. 98–99.

NASTURTIUM

LEAF MINERS

Symptoms: Fine tracery over leaves.
Solution: Try a tansy antifeedant spray. In bad cases use pyrethrum spray; spray with oil in temperatures below 20°C, or with soapy water.

PANSY

POWDERY MILDEW

Solution: Pansies need good air circulation, so should be planted in raised beds.

PEONY

BOTRYTIS LEAF AND FLOWER SPOT

Symptoms: Water-soaked spots on flowers, slimy petals, small, reddish leaf spots that turn large and brown. Stems may rot.
Solution: Remove any diseased or spent plants. Spray with chamomile tea, or double-strength garlic, elder or casuarina sprays.

FAILURE TO FLOWER

Symptoms: Rotted buds and foliage.
Solution: Improve air circulation; keep mulch away from plants during flowering. Spring in your area may be too hot or too short to allow proper flower development. Peonies usually need several years to establish.

PERENNIAL PHLOX

VIRUSES

Symptoms: Green flowers.
Solution: Remove and burn infected plants. Do not replant for at least three years.

PHLOX DRUMMONDII

EXCESS NITROGEN

Symptoms: White or transparent leaves, failure to flower well.
Solution: Mulch with a low-nitrogen mulch such as wood chips or oat hay.

POLYANTHUS

MEALY BUGS

Symptoms: Plants wilt, growth is stunted.
Solution: Control ants with companion plants of wormwood or tansy. Use a good moist mulch such as lucerne or hen manure. Practise crop rotation, and encourage natural controls such as ladybirds, lacewing larvae and chalcid parasitic wasps. Prune affected foliage; try an oil spray in temperatures below 20°C or a soapy water spray at night.

POPPY

MILDEW
Symptoms: White film over leaves.
Solution: See Zucchini, p. 94.

VIRUSES
Symptoms: Enlarged buds that fail to open; yellow-lined leaves.
Solution: Burn affected plants; do not replant in the same place.

WIND DAMAGE
Symptoms: Twisted stems.
Solution: Mulch thickly; lucerne is excellent.

PORTULACA

COLLAR ROT
Symptoms: Plants wilt and die.
Solution: Avoid overwatering; make sure all organic matter in the soil is well decomposed. If the problem persists, plant in new soil.

SNAPDRAGON

SEEDLING BLIGHT
Symptoms: Young seedlings develop rotted stems and leaves and suddenly die.
Solution: Avoid planting in sodden ground; make sure soil is well-drained and contains no undecomposed organic matter. Pull out affected seedlings and drench the rest of the plants in double-strength chamomile tea.

SHOT HOLE
Symptoms: Brown or transparent circles in foliage.
Solution: Spray with Bordeaux in winter, or with chamomile or chive tea, elder or casuarina spray at any time.

SNAPDRAGON RUST
Symptoms: Reddish-brown spots on leaves and stem.
Solution: See *Bellis perennis*, pp. 98–99.

STOCK

BACTERIAL ROT
Symptoms: Brown, wilted leaves; blackened stems.
Solution: See Rust under *Bellis Perennis*, pp. 98–99. Ensure infected stock doesn't seed.

VIRUSES
Symptoms: Streaked flowers.
Solution: Dig out plants and burn; control aphids to stop virus spreading; do not replant in the same area.

SWEET PEA

FAILURE TO FLOWER
This can occur in excessive heat, very cold weather or on overcast days.

MILDEW
Symptoms: Grey film over leaves.
Solution: See Zucchini, p. 94.

ROOT AND STEM FUNGI
Symptoms: Plants suddenly wilt and die.
Solution: Avoid planting in humid conditions or drench the ground in chamomile tea if planting in humid weather. Make sure there is no undecomposed organic matter in the soil. A mulch of lucerne, comfrey, yarrow, nettles, chives or garlic tops is excellent, but don't place too close to the stems.

VIRUSES
Symptoms: Brown, paper-like leaves.
Solution: These may be transferred from broad beans; do not grow the two plants close together. Remove affected plants and burn.

VIOLET

RED SPIDER MITES
Symptoms: Fine, yellow mottling on leaves.
Solution: Water well in spring and summer; overhead water in hot dry weather. Try oil

spray in temperatures below 20°C or soapy water spray in temperatures below 24°C, or anise or coriander sprays. Encourage predators such as thrips, ladybirds and lacewing larvae. See Aster, p. 98.

VIOLET SCAB

Symptoms: Small water-soaked spots which enlarge into grey–brown scabby patches: dead material in the centre falls out, leaving holes.
Solution: Remove affected parts of the plant. Spray with elder, horsetail, double-strength garlic sprays, chamomile tea, or a combination of all of them. Aspirin or seaweed spray every two weeks will improve resistance.

ZINNIA

FLOWER GRUBS

Symptoms: Tunnels in flowers.
Solution: Apply Dipel or derris or pyrethrum spray mixed with a little soapy water to help the spray stick.

FUNGUS WILT

Symptoms: Plants wilt and darken.
Solution: Pull up affected plants and burn; drench area with casuarina tea.

POWDERY MILDEW

Symptoms: Powdery patches on foliage.
Solution: See *Bellis perennis*, pp. 98–99.

BULBS, CORMS AND RHIZOMES

• Use only fat, firm bulbs which have a pleasant smell.

• Bulbs need very little feeding. A thin scatter of blood and bone once a year after flowering is plenty. Use fertiliser that is high in phosphorous. Over-fed plants become soft and disease-prone.

• Plant bulbs at a depth of one to three times the size of the bulbs. (Higher plantings may result in earlier flowers.)

• Avoid digging around bulbs; this may damage them and cause them to rot.

• Bulbs need well-drained soil that is slightly moist, never wet.

• If naturalised bulbs are a problem in strong-growing lawns, plant earlier varieties.

• Make sure any organic matter in the soil near the growing bulbs is well-rotted.

• Do not bend or cut off bulbs' foliage, as the foliage produces food for next year. Leave it to die back.

FAILURE TO FLOWER

This may be caused by an overly shaded position (light requirements vary with different bulbs). It may also be the result of, cutting off foliage the previous year, or of overcrowding, as bulb numbers gradually increase.

In warm areas some bulbs, such as tulips, need a period of chilling in the fridge to flower. Make sure they are planted out into cool soil.

Very small bulbs may simply be too tiny. Let them gradually increase to flowering size.

Bulbs can rot in very wet weather if there is poor drainage, or if they have been planted too deep.

MAJOR PESTS AND DISEASES

APHIDS
Symptoms: Various aphids feed on and damage bulbs; they can sometimes be found in the dry outer skins. Flowers that develop after aphid infestation are small or distorted.
Solution: Take off any easily peeled outer layers on planting. Use healthy bulbs.

BACTERIAL SOFT ROT
Symptoms: Rotting bulbs at ground level.
Solution: Improve drainage; channel away surface water; make sure any organic matter incorporated in the soil is well-rotted.

BULB MITES
Symptoms: Round, yellow-white mites with brown legs infest bulbs, sometimes totally destroying them, or producing plants with yellow and distorted leaves.
Solution: Separate bulbs from each other in storage with crumpled newspaper. If mites have been a problem the previous season, sterilise them. Heat water to 49°C; dip bulbs into the water in a wire basket. Let temperature drop to 43°C. Keep them at this temperature for 4 hours, or 4½ hours for larger bulbs.

BULB NEMATODES
Symptoms: Brown rings of rot inside bulbs.
Solution: Keep bulbs separated in storage, on wire racks or with newspaper between them.

CATERPILLARS
Symptoms: Foliage or flowers eaten.
Solution: Pick off by hand; use Dipel or derris spray; encourage predators.

MILLIPEDES
Symptoms: These are long, thin, black or brown and segmented. Millipedes may curl into flat spirals if disturbed. They may invade houses but will probably not attack plants.

Solution: Millipedes do little harm unless numbers build up; for this they need moist conditions with high levels of organic matter in the soil. Remove mulch if millipedes are badly damaging bulbs. A thin scatter of talcum powder will repel millipedes.

SLATERS
Symptoms: These are a flat, oval shape, and grey, brown or reddish-orange in colour. They do not usually attack plants.
Solution: If slaters are a problem, clear up old wood piles, slow compost heaps and piles of vegetation, etc., where they may be breeding.

SLUGS AND SNAILS
Symptoms: Foliage and flowers eaten.
Solution: See Slugs and snails, pp. 48–49.

SPRINGTAILS
Symptoms: These are small, soft, white to grey insects, 2 mm long. If disturbed, they may run or jump. Springtails feed on decaying organic matter and damaged or diseased plants but should not generally be a problem.
Solution: Clear up wood piles, slow compost heaps, etc.; keep plants growing strongly. If springtails build up to plague proportions, try drying out the soil or adding lime.

THRIPS
Symptoms: Mottled leaves or distorted flowers.
Solution: Heavy rain or hot dry weather should reduce thrip populations. Try strong jets of (preferably hot) water or a soapy water spray on foliage. Try onion spray on flowers and foliage. Plant flowering ground covers nearby to lure thrips away and to control winter-flowering weeds that may harbour them.

VIRUSES
Symptoms: Irregular, pale green or yellow patterns on leaves.
Solution: Dig out affected plants and destroy them. Control aphids which can carry viruses.

PROBLEMS

AGAPANTHUS

FAILURE TO FLOWER

Solution: Agapanthus can take several years to flower. The area may also be too shady or the fertiliser too rich in nitrogen. Agapanthus will thrive with almost no feeding at all.

ALLIUM

APHIDS

Symptoms: Distorted flowers.
Solution: Spray with soapy water, or repeated applications of pyrethrum. See Aphids, p. 105.

AMARYILLIS

FAILURE TO FLOWER

This can be due to the plants' immaturity or the clumps being planted too deep. They flower best when left undisturbed.

ANEMONE

APHIDS

Symptoms: Distorted flowers.
Solution: Spray with soapy water. Grow wormwood, tansy, marigolds or lavender nearby as a deterrent. See Aphids, p. 105.

CANNA

STEM BORER GRUBS

Symptoms: Stems collapse.
Solution: Cut out affected plants; spray the others with pyrethrum.

CROCUS

FAILURE TO FLOWER

Mild winters may cause this.

DAFFODIL

BASAL ROT

Symptoms: Yellow, twisted foliage (this may also be caused by eelworm or mites).
Solution: Plant again in well-drained soil; make sure organic matter in the soil is properly decomposed.

FREESIA

BROWN OR SHRIVELLED LEAVES

Solution: This can be due to too much water or too much high-nitrogen fertiliser.

FUSARIUM WILT

Symptoms: Dying tips with streaks continuing down the leaves.
Solution: Don't plant soggy or blackened bulbs; dig out affected plants; cover soil with clear plastic for a month to kill off spores. Try a triple-strength garlic spray on the soil around the plants and on the plants themselves.

GLADIOLUS

FAILURE TO FLOWER

The bulbs may be too small.

UNOPENED FLOWER HEADS

These are probably due to thrips, as are white flecks at the base of the foliage and brown leaf tips (the latter may also be caused by damage to the bulbs or too much nitrogenous fertiliser). See Thrips, p. 105.

GINGER

STEM BORERS

Symptoms: Leaves and stems wilt.
Solution: Cut out affected plants; other

controls are not very effective because the borer is protected in the stems.

HIPPEASTRUM

FAILURE TO FLOWER
Poor growing conditions in the previous season may cause this. Bulbs may have been planted too deep or slugs or snails may have damaged the buds. See Slugs and snails, pp. 48–49.

IRIS

FUNGUS LEAF SPOT
Symptoms: Purple-brown spots on leaves.
Solution: Spray with Bordeaux in temperatures below 24°C; try chamomile tea at any time, or horsetail tea mixed with double-strength garlic spray.

NYMPHEA (WATER LILY)

WEEVILS OR GRUBS
Symptoms: Chewed foliage.
Solution: Push leaves underwater with wire netting or sticks for a few days so that fish and other predators eat the insects.

ORCHID

ANTS
Solution: These may be seeking the sugary excretions of aphids; if so, control the aphids. Orchids themselves may be sweet enough to attract ants. Grease-band the base of the plant or the pot to stop ants climbing up, or use a talcum powder barrier.

DENDROBIUM BEETLES
Symptoms: Canes or foliage eaten, sometimes with only tougher veins remaining.
Solution: This oval, orange beetle is about 8 mm long with dark patches at the wing tips. The larvae may cause considerable damage by tunnelling through the plant. The beetles can be found on the leaves or new growth, or resting (well camouflaged) on the base of the flower lip. Pick them off by hand, squash and make bug juice.

TRILLIUM

FAILURE TO FLOWER
This may be due to warm or dry weather; trilliums need moist, cool soil.

TULIP

Tulip bulbs should be dug as soon as foliage yellows, and stored in temperatures between 18°C and 25°C until planting time. Tulips start to grow when the temperature is below 10°C; any great rise in temperature will kill them. If you are chilling tulips in the fridge, make sure they are planted out into cool soil.

VIRUSES
Symptoms: These vary and include pale yellow mottling between veins, circular black spots, and irregular sunken patches on leaves.
Solution: Destroy all infected plants.

POT PLANTS

Most pot plants die because we fail to realise they are living creatures, not ornaments. Pot plants have needs and preferences and if we don't look after them and put them in the right position, they wither and die. Too often we buy the gaudiest, most floriferous pot plants in the shop; these have often been forced (heavily fed with artificial fertiliser) to look spectacular and even with the best of care may never look as good again (if they survive to the next season). Flowering pot plants may last only a few weeks indoors. For example, chrysanthemums need to be planted out when the blooms die back and annual primulas will die naturally when their season comes to an end.

CHOOSING HARDY POT PLANTS:

• Look for tough-leafed plants.

• Look for plants with established root systems. (Forced plants rarely have large roots.)

• Look for dusty plants on back shelves; if they have survived neglect at the nursery, they may survive your black fingers, too.

• If in doubt, ask. Good nurseries should have someone available to advise you on the hardiest pot plants in stock.

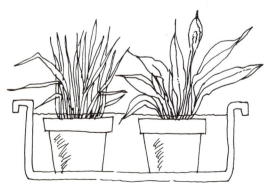

Leaching out fertiliser

CARING FOR POT PLANTS

WATERING

Don't overwater. More plants die from too much water than from too little. Let pot soil dry out to the 'just damp' stage before watering. Cold pot plants do best if they are slightly dry, so reduce watering in winter.

FEEDING

Feeding house plants is an art. Underfed plants either die slowly or go gradually paler. Overfed plants die more quickly, with burnt-off roots or withered, brown-edged leaves. Most newly purchased pot plants have probably already been given a slow release feed and do not need feeding for at least several months.

Feed plants only when they are growing new flowers or new leaves. Most house plants fail to grow much because of imperfect temperature and lack of light; they simply will not use very much fertiliser. Soak pot plants overnight to leach out excess harmful salts in fertilisers.

Be careful with fertiliser granules. Most start to break down and release their fertiliser only in warm weather; if you've fertilised in autumn and then in spring, the plant may be suddenly overloaded and the roots burned with too much harsh feeding. Never give more than the recommended dose of a proprietary fertiliser.

REPOTTING

If roots start poking out the bottom of the pot and leaves are getting smaller and paler, the plant needs repotting. Most house plants grow slowly, however, and will survive a crowded pot for years. When repotting, soak the old pot well, gently heave out the plant and tease the roots so they point outwards. Soak the

Leaf galls are usually a cosmetic problem only but can be controlled by pruning;
spray new growth on ornamentals and blueberries with Bordeaux as a pest-repellent.

To minimise lawn beetle damage, topdress the lawn with compost; this will encourage predacious insects and
microorganisms. Large birds such as kookaburras and magpies will eat lawn beetle larvae.

Companion planting with marigolds can help deter sap-sucking pests. The flowers can also be made into a pesticide which is especially effective on aphids.

A border of comfrey will keep couch and kikuyu out of your garden and also makes good homegrown mulch.

new pot with its extra soil overnight to 'settle' it, and do not feed for a couple of months to encourage roots to explore the new soil. If the plant is temperamental, place a plastic bag over the whole pot for a week or two to increase humidity until the roots recover (or fine mist the leaves a few times a day).

CLEANING

Wipe the leaves, stems and shoots with a damp, very slightly soapy wettex. Regular cleaning removes dust (enabling plants to breathe) and any sap-sucking pests such as scale or mites.

AIRING

Don't put pot plants in direct sunlight as the leaves may shrivel, burn or die. Keep in semi-shade. If the plants wilt or the leaves get paler and smaller, take them indoors at once.

POTS

Grow pot plants in any container with drainage: plastic bottles with a few skewer holes, tin cans with holes punched in them, etc.

MAJOR PESTS AND DISEASES

APHIDS

Symptoms: Small insects clustered mostly on new growth; leaves or flowers are distorted.
Solution: Place pots outside for a few weeks to encourage predators; wipe leaves with a soapy wettex; spray with a seaweed and nettle spray; try lantana, onion or pyrethrum sprays.

CATERPILLARS

Symptoms: Holes in foliage.
Solution: Spray with Dipel or pick them off by hand; try white pepper spray.

COLLAR ROT

Symptoms: Stem decay at plant base.

Solution: By the time collar rot is noticeable it may be too late to save the plant. If possible, take cuttings of uninfected material. Try scraping off dead outer layers, down to the firm material, taking off as little as possible to avoid ringbarking. Drench the plant in undiluted garlic spray. Avoid overwatering in future and make sure potting mix drains well. If possible, remove the plant from its old pot, wash off all soil, drench roots with garlic spray, then repot in clean soil.

LEAF EELWORMS

Symptoms: Wedge-shaped brown or black areas on leaves, usually followed by shrivelling.
Solution: Drench pot with a solution of 1 part molasses to 9 parts water to dehydrate eelworms, then soak in clean water for 12 hours; maintain levels of organic matter; mulch with compost or repot in good well-rotted compost or worm manure.

MEALY BUGS

Symptoms: Downy, white patches on foliage or stems, possibly followed by sooty mould.
Solution: Dip pots in water for a few hours to drown bugs, then control with grease bands at the base of the plant; prune affected foliage or wipe leaves on top and bottom with a soapy wettex or, if temperatures are below 20°C, a wettex dipped in oil spray.

MITES

Symptoms: Foliage is distorted and thickened, may be dull and pitted, and sometimes has skeletonised traces over it.
Solution: Use milk spray; wipe leaves with a soapy wettex.

POWDERY AND DOWNY MILDEW

Symptoms: Powdery or greyish film over foliage.
Solution: Pick off affected foliage as soon as symptoms appear; spray with chive or chamomile tea, milk or garlic spray. Try to

reduce humidity; remove plant from hot, wet areas such as the kitchen and away from other plants that need frequent watering.

Too much high-nitrogen fertiliser promotes soft, sappy growth that is susceptible to mildews. Place the pot in fresh water for 10 minutes to leach out the excess nitrogen, then use a seaweed or fish fertiliser instead.

ROOT ROTS

Symptoms: Plant may wilt or collapse.
Solution: If no more than 20% of the roots have been destroyed, try to save the plant. Take the plant from the pot, remove as much soil as possible from the roots and trim off any dead or broken roots. Dip the remaining roots in undiluted garlic spray. Repot using a clean mix. If unsure about soil sterility, cook in the oven with a medium-sized raw potato until the potato is cooked. Any pathogens should by then be destroyed. A good root rot-killing potting mix is made from a compost of equal parts lucerne and wattle tree bark, plus a little decomposed hen manure. Feed with a foliar spray until roots recover.

Use a potting mix which has less clay to provide better drainage. Never put undecomposed organic matter in a potting mix; it is excellent on top if it does not touch the plant's stem.

SCALE

Symptoms: Small encrustations on leaves or stem; these may be black, green, red or brown, flat, raised or pin-sized.
Solution: Crush scale between your fingers; wipe leaves with a soapy wettex, or leave the plant outside for a couple of weeks to encourage predators.

WHITEFLIES

Symptoms: Many tiny white flies clustered round plant; foliage may be mottled.
Solution: Whiteflies are worse when soil is deficient in phosphorous or magnesium. Add dolomite, ground rock phosphate or wood ash to the soil. Put pot outdoors on a mild day to encourage predators. Rhubarb in pots is said to help deter whiteflies from greenhouses. Wipe foliage with a soapy wettex.

GENERAL SYMPTOMS OF POOR CONDITION

PLANTS SHRINK

Plants with too much or too little light will wither away. Place in a better position; near a window, or away from one, depending on the plant's preferences.

SPOTS ON FOLIAGE

This may be due to water marks; try not to water foliage. If it's dusty, wipe with a damp wettex. Use only room-temperature water, not cold from the tap.

FAILURE TO FLOWER

This is often due to insufficient light, too much light or uneven watering. Plants may also have been given too much high-nitrogen fertiliser. Leach it out by placing the pot in fresh water for 10 minutes. Sometimes pot plants will flower if you place them near a bowl of fruit for a few weeks.

YELLOW OR DROPPING LEAVES

This is probably caused by nitrogen deficiency. Feed the plant with a proprietary seaweed or fish fertiliser. Leaf drop may also be caused by too much or too little light, cold or heat, or over-feeding.

BUD DROP

This can be due to a sudden change in temperature, especially in a room that is heated during the day but gets very cold at night, or if the pot is in a draught. Bud drop can also be caused by low humidity. Keep a saucer of water nearby, or place with other pots, or place in a moist environment such as above the sink or in the bathroom, or spray daily with a mister.

Plants may have root damage or too much salt in the mix. If this is the case it is likely that plants will be stunted, wilting or dying.

LEAF DROP

This is usually caused by insufficient light or sudden falls or fluctuations in temperature. Move plant to a better-lit, draught-proof area and water with room temperature water only. Leaf drop may also be caused by high concentrations of salts in the potting mix; leach out in fresh water for a couple of hours.

Occasionally leaf drop occurs because of gaseous pollution; if the pot is near a gas stove or cylinder, check for leaks. Ethylene produced by apples ripening in a nearby fruit bowl may also cause leaf drop in a pot plant.

FOLIAGE ROLLING UPWARDS

This happens naturally in some plants, especially at night or with insufficient light; it can also be caused by draughts.

FREQUENT WILTING

This can be due to underwatering or hot weather. The plant may be pot-bound, have root disease, or have had too much fertiliser. If you suspect the latter, place it in fresh water for 10 minutes to leach some of it out.

BROWN LEAF TIPS

Make sure the water isn't salty or high in chlorine or fluoride. If one of these is the case, place pots in fresh water for a couple of hours to leach the excess salts. Brown tips may also be caused by dry soil or a dry atmosphere. Make sure plants have enough water, and improve humidity by placing saucers of water or other pot plants nearby. Tips may also brown off in hot weather. Move the plants to a cooler spot, provide better ventilation or spray daily.

WHITE ENCRUSTATIONS ON THE SOIL

This is probably caused by excess salts in the potting mix. All water contains some dissolved salts and in pots (especially frequently watered pots) there is nowhere for the salts to leach to. Repot into clean potting mix or soak in fresh water for 20 minutes to leach out salts.

INSUFFICIENT LIGHT

Plants show this in various ways: failure to flower, a strong tendency to lean towards the lighted area, thin straggly growth, yellowish or faded foliage.

TOO MUCH LIGHT

Indoor plants with too much light are often stumpy, with a clumped look; leaves may yellow and fall.

PROBLEMS

AFRICAN VIOLET

FAILURE TO FLOWER

Solution: This may be due to poor light or insufficient phosphorous. Move the plant closer to a window but not too near the glass. Water with green manure water (see p. 4) or liquid compost (see p. 15).

MITES

Symptoms: Clumped, distorted foliage.
Solution: See Mites, p. 109.

TOO LITTLE LIGHT

Symptoms: Leaves are long and thin.

TOO MUCH LIGHT

Symptoms: Short leaves, clumped together.

WATER MARKS
Symptoms: Pale rings, streaks or patches.
Solution: Use only room temperature water, not tap water. Try to keep water off the leaves.

ANTHURIUM

FAILURE TO FLOWER
This is probably due to poor light.

ASPARAGUS FERN

LEAF DROP
Solution: Give more light, especially in warm weather or if the house is heated.

AZALEA

FAILURE TO FLOWER
Put azaleas outside as soon as flowering is over. See Azalea under Trees and shrubs, p. 117.

BEGONIA

MILDEW
Symptoms: Dark, shrivelled leaves.
Solution: Place plant in better ventilation, away from rain or sprinklers. Drench plant and pot in chamomile tea.

BEGONIA (TUBEROUS)

LEAF AND BUD DROP
This is caused by high temperatures and poor air circulation. Begonias are best suited to rooms where temperatures are below 30°C. Begonia leaves naturally drop and wither after flowering.

CACTUS

FAILURE TO FLOWER
This may be due to lack of bright light. Cacti may also fail to flower if they have been too warm in winter, often the case in heated houses. Put them outside for a few months in midwinter. Cacti should be allowed to almost dry out between waterings.

Strap or jungle cacti need at least six weeks each year of at least 12 hours per day of darkness; keep them away from lighted rooms.

TOO LITTLE LIGHT
Symptoms: Cacti fail to flower; growth may be uneven, falling towards the lighted side; growth may be thin and straggly.

TOO MUCH WATER
Symptoms: Failure to flower; rotting stem.
Solution: Take a cutting of healthy tissue; let it dry out for 12 hours, then plant it in clean potting mix.

CALADIUM

SHRIVELLED OR YELLOW LEAVES
This may be caused by insufficient light, overwatering, or temperatures below 18°C.

CAMELLIA

FAILURE TO FLOWER
If camellias receive insufficient light, foliage becomes thin and elongated and the plant will fail to flower. See also Camellia under Trees and shrubs, p. 118.

CHLOROPHYTUM (SPIDER PLANT)

BROWN LEAF TIPS
Chlorine in the water and an overly dry atmosphere may contribute to this problem.
Solution: Improve humidity.

CLIVEA

BROWN LEAF TIPS
Solution: Avoid direct sunlight.

COLUMNEA

FAILURE TO FLOWER

Columneas will fail to flower without long nights and temperatures between 13°C and 18°C. Beware of heated, artificially lit rooms.

CORDYLINE

BROWN PATCHES ON LEAVES

These may be caused by a build-up of fluoride from the water or by perlite in the potting mix.
Solution: Repot in clean mixture.

CYCLAMEN

BUD DROP AND YELLOW FOLIAGE

This may be caused by high night temperatures.
Solution: Move the pot to a cooler place. Reduce watering when foliage yellows naturally after flowering.

CYCLAMEN MITES

Symptoms: Clumped, distorted foliage.
Solution: See Mites, p. 109.

FERN

Some natural symptoms in ferns are often taken as a sign of disease. Brown scale-like clusters under the leaves are the natural spores and indicate that the plant is growing well, not that it is infected. Some fern foliage naturally shrivels and dies to make way for new leaves, but if all the foliage browns, it may be caused by humidity or lack of water.

APHIDS

Symptoms: Small insects on new shoots.
Solution: See Aphids, p. 109.

LEAF EELWORMS

Symptoms: Wedge-shaped brown or black areas that subsequently shrivel.
Solution: See Eelworms, p. 109.

LEAF HOPPERS (JASSIDS)

Symptoms: Mottled fronds, especially on tree ferns.
Solution: Wipe with a soapy wettex; use garlic spray.

MUSHROOM FLIES

Symptoms: Many tiny black insects hovering round plant.
Solution: This may be caused by mushroom compost in the potting mix. Spray plant with pyrethrum; if possible soak the pot for a day in a solution of 1 part pyrethrum to 9 parts water.

SCALE

Symptoms: Brown, dome-shaped scales.
Solution: See Scale, pp. 115–16.

STAGHORN BEETLES

Symptoms: Small brown indentations in leaves; larvae tunnel and fronds shrivel.
Solution: Spray backs of leaves and centre of plant thoroughly with bug juice, or garlic or wormwood sprays. Try a tansy antifeedant spray.

WHITEFLIES

Symptoms: Masses of tiny white flies clustered round plant; foliage may be mottled.
Solution: See Whiteflies, p. 110.

FICUS

LEAF DROP

This may occur if the environment is suddenly changed or if the room temperature is too high for the amount of light available.

FITTONIA

STEM ROT

Symptoms: Plants rot at ground level.
Solution: Water fittonias only when the soil is almost dry. Discard rotten plants and take cuttings from healthy growth on the top.

FUCHSIA

LEAF DROP
Gradual leaf drop is natural in lower temperatures or if there is insufficient light or water. Never use pyrethrum on fuchsias as it causes severe leaf drop.

GLOXINIA

POOR FLOWERING
This is usually the result of insufficient light.

SHRIVELLED LEAF MARGINS
This is often due to low humidity.

HIPPEASTRUM

NARCISSUS MITES
Symptoms: Distorted flowers and foliage; reddish stains at base of leaves.
Solution: See Mites, p. 109.

HOYA

FAILURE TO FLOWER
This may occur in immature plants or plants in poorly lit positions or because the last lot of flower heads was removed.

PALM

Palms' lower leaves naturally wither and die as new ones emerge. The new fronds of phoenix palms are sometimes fused together with a whitish down; this is also natural. Palms usually die from root damage, which can happen during repotting and may be unnoticeable for some time. Handle palms gently. Beware of overfeeding, which can also kill them; feed with a very weak liquid manure only when new growth appears. Water only when the soil is nearly dry.

DOWNY SCALE
Symptoms: Small, downy scales on foliage, yellow blotches on underside.
Solution: Wipe with a soapy wettex.

PALM LEAF-ROLLING CATERPILLAR
Symptoms: Foliage eaten.
Solution: Leave outdoors for predators to attack the pest; wipe the plant all over with a soapy wettex; try Dipel; pick off by hand.

PALM SCALE
Symptoms: This produces tiny, tan scales on leaves, with yellow blotches on the undersides.
Solution: Wipe with a soapy wettex.

OTHER PALM PROBLEMS
Brown tips. This is caused by dry air; improve humidity.
Large brown patches. This often happens if plants are placed near heaters or in sudden sunlight after shade.
Irregular blotches on leaf margins. This is caused by root damage, overfeeding, or wet soil. To correct overfeeding, soak the pot in water for an hour, then allow to dry out.
Dull leaves. These may be caused by root damage or overdry soil.

POINSETTIA

FAILURE TO FLOWER
This occurs if plants are kept in artificial light.

TREES AND SHRUBS

MAJOR PESTS AND DISEASES

SCALE

Scale appears as small, scaly encrustations. Scale infestations can wither young shoots, creating brown leaves and split bark and general loss of vigour in bushes and trees. Scale sucks up the contents of plant cells and, in some cases, injects toxins into the plant. Like all sap-suckers, scale excretes large quantities of honeydew, which encourages sooty mould.

There are over 500 species of scale in Australia, both native and introduced (the cochineal scale, for example, was introduced to help control prickly pear). Most can be identified only with a magnifying glass. Some, such as the armoured scale, have hard protective covers; adults of the soft varieties, such as waxy scale, have tough or waxy tops.

MAIN TYPES OF SCALE

Black scale appears on evergreen trees and bushes as well as on melon and pumpkin foliage. Oleander, hibiscus, gardenias, perennial daisies and passionfruit can be affected. Sooty mould is the worst effect of black scale.

Red scale is a major citrus pest, particularly in dusty orchards where the leaves have a light film on them. Sometimes leaving a grass cover under trees instead of ploughing can drastically reduce red scale. Red scale injects a toxic saliva as it feeds and trees can suffer a lot of damage quickly; yellow, falling leaves, splitting bark, dying twigs and branches.

San José scale is hard to see, because it is much the same colour as the twigs it feeds on, but it will feel rough if you run your fingers over it. It can also be seen with the aid of a magnifying glass. San José scale affects stone fruit, apples, pears, tree lucerne, willows and other ornamentals, and often plagues organic (and other) orchardists in spring.

Wax scale infests evergreen fruit trees such as citrus, mango and guava, as well as persimmons, pears, quinces and a range of ornamentals. Wax scale produces honeydew; in humid conditions the black, sooty smudges of sooty mould are almost inevitable.

White louse scale is another major citrus pest, mostly on trunks of mature trees. Twigs and even branches die back. Plagues are usually obvious; the scale looks like white lice. crouched on the trunk.

NATURAL SCALE CONTROLS

1. Reduce sprays that may kill off predators. There are often large increases in scale populations after the use of organophosphate poisons and also after Bordeaux spray. This copper-based spray is commonly used by organic growers in winter for such problems as curly leaf, shot hole, bacterial blights and brown rot. Copper-based sprays will also kill off ladybirds, which is one reason for the early spring build-up of scale in many orchards.

Avoid using Bordeaux in late winter; try several earlier sprays instead, or spray every second tree only. Wait ten days, then spray the rest. This way some predators will survive to breed and spread.

2. Encourage native and other diverse species. These will harbour predators and colonies of scale to feed them. As in all natural pest control, encourage *some* pests to feed your predators and avoid a population explosion.

3. Avoid windbreaks of osage orange, japonica, hawthorn and tree lucerne near orchards. These are major hosts of San José scale.

4. Try to keep ants at bay if black or brown scale are present. Ants also deter wasps from gathering scale. Place grease-bands round the trunks of trees and shrubs so ants can't climb up. Grow rue, tansy or wormwood at the base of trees.

5. Keep plants growing strongly. Insect pests seem to be attracted to unthrifty trees; healthy trees are able to withstand scale damage until predators start to control the pest. At the same time, avoid high-nitrogen fertilisers and overwatering; anything that encourages soft, sappy growth will only encourage scale (and other pests).

6. Encourage predators. Natural predators of scale include introduced and native wasps, ladybirds and their larvae, lacewing larvae and a small, blue, metallic-looking fly, *Cryptochaelum icerae*. Bees sometimes remove scales' waxy coating in spring. Birds are particularly good scale gatherers, especially eastern spinebills, silvereyes, yellow-tailed thornbills, pardalotes and many others. See Birds, p. 44.

7. Don't dig around the trees and shrubs. Dusty plants are more susceptible to scale.

Other controls:
• Knock scale off with a toothbrush or wire brush, or squash them between your fingers.

• Gather scale to make bug juice. As it is hard to collect scale without collecting leaves too, allow for the leaf mass when adding water. Blend scale in a sieve or blender, add an equal amount of tepid milk (most recipes use water but milk is more effective), leave 24 hours and spray. This recipe supposes that the scale will find their squashed comrades unattractive, or

that one of the squashed scale may be host to a disease or parasite and the bug juice will help spread it.

• Try spreading diluted clay; this suffocates the scale. Use just enough pure clay to dirty the water.

• White oil or home-made oil sprays are a traditional remedy: use these as a last resort because they also kill some of the scale predators. As with Bordeaux, if you must spray, spray only every second tree, wait ten days, and spray again. Oil sprays should be used in late winter or early spring. Do not use them when the temperature is above 24°C, or the foliage will burn. If in any doubt spray in the evening or in dull weather. Never use oil spray on blossom or on fruit, as they will be damaged. Oil sprays work by covering insects with a film of oil that suffocates them. The same principle works with soapy water and clay spray but oil spray is more persistent, thorough and effective.

• Try soapy water or sprays of mustard, onion, glue, garlic, quassia or pyrethrum. For plants such as rose bushes, try an occasional cleaning with an old toothbrush and soapy water.

• Ensure that your garden has healthy trees, lots of birds and other species.

SOOTY MOULD
This affects most ornamentals. Infected plants are covered with black patches that look as though they have been dusted with soot. Sooty mould is often stimulated by the sugary secretions of aphids, mealy bugs or scale; they suck sap and their excretions are sweet and sticky too, making a wonderful breeding ground for sooty mould. Eliminate these pests and the problem should clear although it may take a few months for the sooty mould to peel off. Be wary of plants that produce a lot of sweet sap, as do many wattles. Never plant a mould-prone plant under wattles.

Once pests have been controlled try hosing the plant vigorously, with hot water if possible, to keep the mould flake away. A damp, slightly soapy wettex can be used for leaves in reach. Bordeaux spray can be used in temperatures below 24°C but not on tender leaves, buds or flowers.

Sooty mould is usually a problem of position: move the plant to a sunnier spot. Mainly an aesthetic problem, sooty mould may however affect photosynthesis and reduce the vigour of the plant if it covers a wide area for a long time. It can also be a symptom of pest damage.

PROBLEMS

ATHEL

Although this tree will tolerate stress from salt, wind, heat, drought and mild frosts, it will die back if stress, or the combination of different stresses, is too severe. Beetle and other insect attack is likely then but will be the result, not the cause, of the tree's condition.

AZALEA AND RHODODENDRON

Azaleas need acid soils and may die back if planted in concrete pots or where there is builder's rubble containing concrete (this makes the soil conditions alkaline). Some azaleas are naturally crevice-growing plants; they like crammed roots and will die in the open garden, although they will thrive in pots. Some azaleas may also die back if their roots get too hot: keep them mulched.

Some azalea problems have similar symptoms but different causes. Brown patches on the leaves may be fungal leaf spot or caused by the azalea leaf miner; use garlic spray for both. If in doubt about azalea symptoms, use azalea spray: 1 part chamomile tea; 1 part garlic spray; 1 part soapy water. Spray once a week.

AZALEA LACE BUG
Symptoms: White, yellow or grey mottling. (This may also be due to thrips, whiteflies or red spider mite.) Azalea lace bugs are shiny, 4 mm long black bugs; the nymphs suck sap, leaving mottled leaves with black, sticky spots.
Solution: See Citrus, pp. 61–65.

LEAF-CHEWING CATERPILLARS
Solution: Try a tansy antifeedant spray; dust with white pepper or talcum powder or pick off by hand; in large areas use Dipel, pikelet, or pyrethrum spray.

LEAF GALL
Symptoms: Galls usually appear on the leaves. They are pale green, thick swellings that develop white patches of spores in wet weather.
Solution: Cut off affected foliage and burn. Spray with horsetail or chive tea if new growth is being formed; seaweed spray applied every two weeks may help prevent leaf gall.

PETAL BLIGHT
Symptoms: Buds and flowers dry out until they are brown and papery. Flowers then remain on the plant until long after unaffected flowers have fallen.
Solution: Cut off affected flowers at once. Spray with chamomile, chive or lilac tea as soon as flowers start to form, or every two days if the problem has arisen before.

POWDERY MILDEW
Symptoms: Circular white patches on leaves.
Solution: See Beetroot, p. 80.

BAY TREE

SCALE

Symptoms: White wax scale produces lumps on stems; pink wax scale produces lumps on leaves and stems.

Solution: Control ants with grease bands at base of tree. See Scale, pp. 115–16.

CAMELLIA

CAMELLIA BUD MITES

Symptoms: Bud drop.

Solution: Control weeds such as capeweed or clover. Try a tansy antifeedant spray. See Red spider mites under Apple, p. 59.

CAMELLIA RUST MITES

Symptoms: Discoloured leaves.

Solution: Frequent overhead watering may control the problem. See Red spider mites under Apple, p. 59.

FAILURE TO FLOWER

This may be caused by sunburn to the buds or flowers while wet, or overwatering or underwatering, poor feeding or poor drainage. Camellias bought in flower may not flower the following year if their roots are badly disturbed. *Camellia japonica* will not flower if it gets too much sun, especially in warm areas.

OEDEMAS

Symptoms: Dark, corky areas on leaves.

Solution: Reduce watering in cloudy weather.

PHYTOPHTHORA ROOT ROT

Symptoms: Dieback. This affects *Camellia japonica* but rarely *Camellia sasanqua*.

Solution: Try to buy *C. japonica* grafted onto *C. sasanqua* rootstock. See Avocado, p. 62.

SUNBURN

Symptoms: Brown patches on the leaves; sun damage on buds or flowers if they are wet with dew. Fungus may colonise damaged areas.

Solution: Provide shade. If necessary transplant to a more suitable spot; even quite large camellias will transplant successfully although they may not flower for a couple of seasons. Camellias have many fine surface feeder roots which resent disturbance so dig around them carefully, but if the root ball can be moved reasonably intact the shrub has a good chance of settling into its new position.

THRIPS

Symptoms: Distorted leaves or flowers.

Solution: See Apple, pp. 59–60.

CYPRESS

CYPRESS BARK WEEVILS

Symptoms: Branches die back; foliage loses colour; larvae chew holes in bark.

Solution: Cut off dead branches; keep plant growing strongly so it can outgrow depredations. The same symptoms may be the result of the cypress pine beetle: control is the same.

CYPRESS CANKER

Symptoms: Dieback of branches; split bark oozing gum.

Solution: Avoid pruning cuts where spores of the fungus can enter. No control is possible when the disease has taken hold; remove the tree and plant another species.

CYPRESS PINE SAWFLIES

Symptoms: Defoliation.

Solution: See Native plants, p. 137.

DAPHNE

SCLEROTINIA ROT

Symptoms: Stem rots at ground level.

Solution: Keep mulch away from the stem.

VIRUSES
Symptoms: Yellow blotches, irregular streaks, distorted flowers that fall prematurely.
Solution: Dig out and burn infected plants; buy virus-resistant cultivars.

FRANGIPANI

DIEBACK
Symptoms: Fleshy stems become hollow, with blackened ends.
Solution: Low temperatures are too low. Insects may invade damaged areas; these are the result, not the cause. A weekly seaweed spray or nettle spray may give some cold resistance.

SCALE
Symptoms: A massed covering of small scales.
Solution: See Scale, pp. 115–16.

FUCHSIA

CYCLAMEN MITES
Symptoms: Small, distorted new shoots.
Solution: Try a tansy antifeedant spray. Try companion planting with marigolds or nasturtiums, or mulch with wormwood. A reflective aluminium foil mulch will keep the pest away temporarily. See Red spider mites under Apple, p. 59.

RUST
Symptoms: Brown patches on the upper leaf surface with orange splotches below.
Solution: Spray with aspirin spray (1 soluble tablet to 1 cup of water), or with Bordeaux in winter. Interplant with chamomile, or try a mulch of comfrey, lucerne, nettles, chives or garlic tops.

WHITEFLIES
Symptoms: Clouds of small, white flies suck at foliage and cluster on shoots.

Solution: Add dolomite, rock phosphate or wood ash to the soil; whiteflies prosper where the soil is deficient in phosphorous or magnesium.

Try growing nasturtiums or marigolds under the bush. Wipe leaves with a soapy wettex; use an oil spray if temperatures are below 24°C; attract whiteflies to yellow boards covered with glue or motor oil. Plant fuchsias in compost or pure worm castings.

GARDENIA

BURNT FLOWERS
This may be caused by growing gardenias in full sun or in dry soil. Choose a semi-shaded spot, and mulch and water regularly.

SCALE
Symptoms: Scaly encrustations on leaves.
Solution: See Scale, pp. 115–16.

THRIPS
Symptoms: Black specks in flowers.
Solution: See Apple, pp. 59–60.

HAWTHORN

PEAR AND CHERRY SLUGS
Symptoms: Skeletonised foliage.
Solution: See Pear and cherry slugs, p. 63.

HIBISCUS

COLLAR ROT
Symptoms: Plant pales, wilts and dies, stem rots at ground level.
Solution: Dig out plant and leave the hole open to the sun for three weeks before replacing with another species. To prevent collar rot, keep mulch away from the base of the hibiscus bush, don't crowd the bush with small nearby plants, don't mow or dig too near the stems.

HIBISCUS BEETLE

These 3 mm long black beetles are mostly pollen feeders, although they may chew holes in petals. There is no need to kill them.

VIRUSES

Symptoms: Yellow flecks on leaves, clear areas on veins.

Solution: Dig out and burn; take cuttings from healthy plants only.

HYDRANGEA

IRON DEFICIENCY

Symptoms: Yellow leaves, pale veins.

Solution: Improve feeding regime; give the plant a regular foliar feed with compost water, green manure or nettle tea until iron deficiency symptoms disappear.

LILAC

BACTERIAL LEAF SPOT

Symptoms: Large black spots on leaves.

Solution: Spray with Bordeaux in winter; use chamomile, lilac or casuarina sprays in summer; regular seaweed sprays or plant tonic will help prevent leaf spot. Feed plants with a good compost or lucerne mulch, or scatter on small amounts of compost regularly if they are growing in the lawn.

FAILURE TO FLOWER

Lilacs may take several years to establish and flower. They will flower in light semi-shade but not in deep shade.

MAPLE

LONGICORN BEETLE LARVAE

Symptoms: These tunnel under the bark, causing it to crack.

Solution: See Borer under Native plants, pp. 125–26.

MONTEREY PINE
(PINUS RADIATA)

SIREX WASPS

These mostly attack poorly growing trees or trees in areas with erratic or low rainfall. Improve feeding.

OLEANDER

OLEANDER BUTTERFLY CATERPILLARS

Symptoms: Chewed leaves.

Solution: Use pikelet or dilute clay spray; dust white pepper on leaves. Try Dipel and encourage birds and other predators. Dust the leaves with derris as a last resort; do not dust the caterpillars as derris is a stomach poison, not a contact killer.

OLEANDER AND OTHER SCALE

Symptoms: Scaly spots on leaves.

Solution: Natural predators should control the problem except in very depleted areas. See Scale, pp. 115–16.

POPLAR

ANTHRACNOSE

Symptoms: Brown patches on leaves.

Solution: Improve air circulation and drainage; prune all affected foliage. Spray with Bordeaux in temperatures below 24°C.

RUST

Symptoms: Yellow flecks on leaves; premature leaf drop.

Solution: Keep plant growing strongly. In bad cases remove and plant another species or try to obtain a rust-resistant variety. Regular sprayings of seaweed spray, soluble aspirin or plant tonic may prevent further outbreaks, but trees are usually too tall for this to be feasible.

SALT TOXICITY

Symptoms: Brown leaf edges.

Solution: Improve water supply if it is contaminated; increase the amount of organic matter in the soil; try to flush out the soil with plenty of fresh water. If water supply is uncertain try to rely on rain; use drip irrigation, not overhead spraying, and only when absolutely necessary.

ROSE

APHIDS

Symptoms: Small green insects on new shoots.

Solution: These are worst in spring because aphids breed early and their predators need warmer weather to build up to sufficient numbers to control them.

Companion planting may be enough to control aphids on roses: try dwarf marigolds, nettles, dwarf nasturtiums, and mustard as a green manure crop in early spring. Try well-trimmed horehound but be careful: this can become a weed and is actually declared noxious in some areas. Wormwood is an excellent aphid repellent; although rose bushes surrounded by wormwood should be more prone to black spot, our roses in wormwood thickets are almost free of it. (They also escape the depredations of wallabies, which love roses but not wormwood thickets.) Pyrethrum and feverfew have a very slight aphid-repelling effect. So do parsley and mint.

A strong hose of water works wonders with aphids, as does squashing them on the infested shoots with your fingers. This may feel messy, but the squashed aphids will repel others.

As a last resort use tansy antifeedant spray, marigold, chilli or pyrethrum sprays. A predacious wasp was released in 1993 for large-scale aphid control on roses and is now commercially available.

BALLING

Symptoms: Flowers ball up and fail to open.

Solutions: This is caused by rain falling on thin-petalled varieties and is worst in shady areas. It can also be caused by a severe aphid infestation.

BLACK SPOT

Symptoms: This is *the* rose disease. In bad cases the whole bush may defoliate and die.

Solution: The most important solution to black spot is to keep roses growing vigorously. Black spot is worse where leaves are unable to dry out, either because the air is naturally humid or because the bushes are surrounded with long grass or tall flowers, or the garden is enclosed in bushes, and where the spores are splashed onto new leaves from last year's plants. Often old leaves will be infected by black spot, but new growth will be healthy.

If your roses are prone to black spot, change your garden design for better air circulation, or better still, move house to a less humid spot (taking your roses with you). Substitute black spot-resistant roses. There are many of these on the market now.

Black spot is worse when there is a potash shortage in the soil; I add wood ash in winter, but most green mulches contain some potash. Compost-fed roses are less prone to black spot and the black spot is less likely to lead to dieback or other serious problems. No matter how good the feeding, black spot can still be a problem. Mulching will also help stop spores splashing up and will stop tall grass and weeds that increase humidity, which makes black spot worse.

Try to avoid overhead watering; just let the hose dribble on the rose bushes instead, preferably under the mulch. Water in the day only as leaves which dry quickly won't develop black spot.

Make sure all of last year's infected leaves are raked up or mulched over. Watch out for sap-suckers such as aphids, as their sweet excretions can stimulate black spot.

In areas with bad black spot problems, spray roses once in winter with Bordeaux mixture or Kocide. Spray all around the bush, especially where there are large thorns. Fortnightly seaweed sprays will help resistance. If black spot appears, spray the leaves (but not the buds or flowers) with half-strength Bordeaux spray, then with strong chamomile tea every week, or baking powder spray (one dessertspoon per litre of water).

CATERPILLARS

Symptoms: Holes in leaves, ragged leaves, large green droppings.

Solution: Encourage birds; pick off by hand or hose off; spray diatomaceous earth (available in Black and Gold kitty litter) mixed with water; sprinkle on dried wood ash or lime in small quantities; try Bordeaux spray or Dipel for caterpillars or use flour on the leaves; as a last resort use derris or pyrethrum spray.

DIEBACK

Symptoms: Dead or dying twigs or branches.

Solution: Shoots can die back after any injury: frost, waterlogging, black spot, etc. Yellow and orange varieties are most susceptible. Dieback usually occurs where the soil is deficient in boron, calcium, potash or phosphorous. In the meantime, cut off the affected shoot below the dead area. To minimise frost damage, do not feed in autumn. Give liquid manure or blood and bone and mulch through spring and early summer.

EARWIGS

Symptoms: Chewed rose buds.

Solution: Grease-band the base so earwigs cannot climb up and eat the buds, or tie on a band of cotton wool dipped in a mixture of derris dust and edible oil. Make earwig traps with balls of crumpled-up newspaper; put these in the garden, and the earwigs will crawl in to shelter. Throw away the old ones and replace with new newspaper balls every day. Earwigs will be a worse problem if you have an old wood pile nearby or if the roses are surrounded with tan bark mulch.

FROST DAMAGE

Symptoms: Leaves are edged with brown, or shrivelled.

Solutions: Do not prune roses too early; late pruning will delay leaf development so that the plant will not be affected by late frosts. In autumn feed with a potash-rich fertiliser, such as comfrey or wood ash, to harden new growth. A calcium-rich spray will also give plants added frost resistance. Buy a commercial calcium spray (these are often used by apple growers to combat bitter pit) or make your own: leave comfrey leaves under water until the water turns dark brown, add an equal amount of seaweed spray, then dilute until the mixture is pale brown. Spray the foliage every three weeks from early spring to early summer, and from early autumn to early winter. See damage control under Frost, pp. 21-23.

MEALY BUGS

Symptoms: Plants wilt; growth is stunted; small, downy, white insects appear under leaves and on roots.

Solution: Common insecticides won't kill mealy bugs because of their protective coating. Prune affected foliage; try an oil spray in cool weather or a soapy water spray at night, or dab on methylated spirits. None of these of these will kill all the pests, but their numbers will be reduced. Probably no complete mealy bug cure exists. As a long-term control, keep ants away with companion plants of wormwood or tansy, or a band of grease around the lower stem; encourage natural controls such as ladybirds, lacewing larvae, chalcid parasitic wasps. Let umbelliferae such as parsnips or fennel flower to increase numbers of parasitic wasps, hoverflies, etc. Avoid over-enthusiastic pruning, as this may attract mealy bugs.

POWDERY MILDEW

Symptoms: Leaves look powdery, pale and blotchy, almost blue.

Solution: Try to improve air circulation around your roses; avoid transferring spores from infected plants to healthy ones; mulch well to stop spores on infected fallen leaves splashing up to reinfect the bush. In cool weather use a washing soda spray, or milk, chamomile or chive teas.

RED SPIDER MITES

Symptoms: Webbing on the leaves.

Solution: Try watering them off. Ensure rose leaves are regularly wet by watering or rain; mites are often a problem where the leaves stay dry. The roots may be getting enough moisture from damp soil but overhanging eaves or other plants may stop the leaves being regularly 'washed'. Pikelet spray is effective; use a pyrethrum spray as a last resort.

Companion planting with marigolds will repel mites if marigolds are flowering, or about to flower when the mites arrive. Once mites get onto a plant they tend to stay there. Borage may also repel mites. Roses grown with comfrey get far fewer mites; comfrey brings up deep-leached nutrients that are returned to the soil when the comfrey leaves decompose in winter, so becoming available for other plants. Plant comfrey around a rose only when the rose is well established (at least four years old) or the comfrey will compete with the young plant.

RUST

Symptoms: Reddish-orange pustules on leaves.

Solution: Rust is encouraged by a shortage of potash, especially after a cool spring. Feed plants with wood ash in autumn, or with a compost or mulch high in comfrey. Spray plants with Bordeaux in winter; use chamomile tea in summer. A spray of 1 soluble aspirin in 1 cup water may also be effective or try meadowsweet tea: 1 cup chopped meadowsweet covered with 2 cups boiling water, left to cool, strained and sprayed.

SALT TOXICITY

Symptoms: Brown leaf edges; roses may be stunted or die.

Solutions: Improve water supply if it is contaminated; add more organic matter to the soil. This will alleviate though not cure the problem; try to flush out the salt with frequent drenchings of clean water.

SCALE

Symptoms: Scaly encrustations on leaves or stems.

Solution: Scale is likely to be a problem on rose bushes that have been sprayed with a fungicide such as Bordeaux or Kocide in winter; the fungicide kills the predators or predator eggs that might help control the scale. Rose bushes in dug garden beds are susceptible to scale because the dust gets onto the predator larvae or eggs and kills them. Scale also seem attracted to bushes that are heavily pruned. Summer pruning cuts heal faster, and there is less time for pests to be attracted.

In trials here with young citrus trees I found that scale was more likely to infest plants fed with high-nitrogen fertiliser than those fed with pelletised hen manure. The scale appeared to ignore trees fed with lucerne mulch or compost. The trees that were not fed were the most heavily scale-infested.

Plant umbelliferae such as parsnips, and let them go to flower to attract scale-eating wasps. Grow parsley under the roses, and let it seed. Flowering parsley is an excellent predator attractor. See Scale, pp. 115–16.

SOOTY MOULD
Symptoms: Affected plants are covered with black patches, which look as though they have been dusted with soot.
Solution: See Sooty mould, pp. 116–17.

THRIPS
Symptoms: Small dark specks in flowers. Flowers fade and fall or fail to open.
Solution: Thrips are a problem of 'desert' gardens where one or two plants or shrubs are the only things flowering. A thrip plague may be caused by digging soil under roses or mowing the lawn. It will occur if the roses are in a patch of annual weeds that have just finished flowering; the thrips move off the weeds onto the roses. Grow plenty of flowering plants at the base of the roses; thrips prefer low-growing flowers and gradually move up. Water these low-growing flowers well; thrips are worse in a dry spring and watering will kill them.

Band the base of the roses with car grease to stop the thrips moving up, or use old wool impregnated with eucalyptus oil. As a last resort, try pyrethrum spray on the flowers.

WATERLOGGING
Symptoms: Leaves are flat and yellowish with yellow veins.
Solution: Dig out the rose and plant it somewhere else, or drain the soil.

YELLOW LEAVES
If the oldest leaves are yellowing, it is nitrogen deficiency; if the young leaves are yellowing, it may be a phosphorous deficiency.
Solution: Feed with good mulch or compost and spray the leaves with liquid manure once a week in the evening until they turn green again. If leaves seem to be yellowing evenly,

check that the plant is neither waterlogged nor starved of water. Rock the plant to see if it seems loose; this would mean root rot. Cold weather will cause leaves to turn yellow. So will herbicide drift. Check the plant base for collar rot or injury from a lawnmower.

UMBRELLA

MEALY BUGS
Symptoms: Blackened or sticky leaves.
Solution: See Rose, p. 122.

SCALE
Symptoms: Black, pink or brown scaly patches.
Solution: See Scale, pp. 115–16.

WHITE CEDAR

WHITE CEDAR MOTH
Symptoms: Defoliation by leaf-eating caterpillars.
Solution: Try Dipel, quassia, garlic and pyrethrum sprays. Encourage birds, wasps and other predators. See Codling moth, pp. 51–53.

WILLOW

RUST
Symptoms: Pale yellow flecks on leaves.
Solution: Prune regularly; new growth is less susceptible to disease.

WILLOW GALL, SAWFLY
Symptoms: Pale green or reddish lumps on leaves.
Solution: Galls are ugly but do not harm the tree. In severe cases use the controls for Sawflies p. 127 and Galls p. 126 under Native plants.

Different rusts affect different plants, so the rust on your willow tree is unlikely to infect other species in the garden. Prune off affected foliage, and spray the plant or tree with soluble aspirin spray.

Protect roses and other shrubs from possums by companion planting with bitter herbs such as wormwood.

Grow seedlings in individual greenhouses made from cut-off plastic bottles
to keep them safe from frost and pests, including snails and cutworms.

NATIVE PLANTS

Generally, native species are more resistant to insect damage than exotics. Many insects feed on native species, but there are also many native predators to control them, as long as poisonous sprays are not used (these will kill off the predators and leave a few poison-resistant pests to breed, then devastate plants next season).

CONTROLS

• Don't apply pest control immediately on sighting a pest. Small numbers of pests may not visibly damage trees and they will provide insurance against greater damage. Wipe out those pests and you may have to re-eradicate them every time they build up.

• Try mechanical means of eradication before applying chemicals or even organic controls (which are toxic to some degree). Mechanical means include picking off pests by hand, traps, suffocating oil or ash sprays, etc.

• If spraying, spray every second plant, wait at least three days, then spray the rest. This way the natural control system is not irrevocably interrupted.

Nectar eaters attracted to banksias and grevilleas will also prey on the moths, the borers or the sawfly that attack plants. Lacewings, hoverflies and certain wasps are useful predators that may be attracted by native blossom. Other predators, such as clerid beetles, which mostly feed on wood borers and tree-living insects, also find native shrubs a perfect habitat.

As with any organic control, always wait to see if predators will do the job before you take control measures. With native plants, you can be certain that just as the pests have evolved with the plants they are eating, so have the predators evolved to prey on the pests.

MAJOR PESTS AND DISEASES

APHIDS, WOOLLY APHIDS, THRIPS
See Avocado, p. 61 and Apple, pp. 59–60.

BEETLES
Beetles can also predate a wide range of pests themselves. Make sure they are actually badly damaging the plant before you control them. They are most easily controlled at the larval stage. See Christmas beetles, p. 126.

BORERS
These are beetle or moth larvae; grubs tunnel into stems or roots and may cause considerable damage, which may not be noticed for some time.

A borer hole with fresh sawdust indicates the borer is still in there; block it off with grafting wax, or skewer the borer out with a bit of wire. Lavender bushes grown around your plants may repel moths.

Sickly trees are more prone to borer attack; healthy trees can engulf the borer with resin as it burrows. Keep trees growing strongly. Paint the trunks and main branches of susceptible plants in early spring with 1 part Bordeaux paste to 4 parts water. This deters the females from laying their eggs on the treated trees.

A simple repellent is a thin slurry of wood ash painted on the tree. In desperate cases try the following repellent: soften 7 kg soap in 4 L water for a few days. Heat until it is too hot to touch, add 0.5 kg flour and 3.5 kg naphthalene flakes. Increase heat and stir until the flakes dissolve. Cool the mixture, then store in an airtight container. Apply warm with a paint brush. This is not an organic remedy because of the naphthalene flakes.

CATERPILLARS (VARIOUS)

The best control for caterpillars of all kinds is birds and wasps, as well as mantises and centipedes. Pick caterpillars off by hand, or dust with powdered clay, white pepper or talcum powder to dehydrate them, or try pikelet spray. As a last resort try derris dust, Dipel or pyrethrum spray.

CHRISTMAS BEETLES

Immature Christmas beetles are large white grubs with reddish heads. They live under the soil particularly where there is lawn or pasture grasses, and eat roots.

In deciduous forests, nutrients are recycled when leaves fall in autumn. In native forests, pests eat the leaves and their droppings and carcasses recycle nutrients so that young plants can grow. Some Christmas beetle damage is good and natural; too much can kill the tree. Christmas beetles usually attack in summer, eating young leaves first and then older ones. They are attracted to gums with pale blue juvenile foliage, and less attracted to strong-smelling species such as lemon-scented gums.

Control. Always interplant eucalypts with other species, especially those that will disguise eucalypts' shapes and attract bird and wasp predators. Scattered trees are most vulnerable. Prune new growth in early summer. Shake the tree and stamp on the beetles. Spray the leaves with garlic, derris, pyrethrum or tomato spray. Do not spray the beetles as their thick carapaces will be relatively unaffected. A fine dusting of diatomaceous earth repels Christmas beetles.

FERN WEEVILS

These eat out stems and pupate in them. Cut out and burn infected fronds or soak them in water for three weeks to break the life cycle.

FUNGI, MILDEWS, SOOTY MOULD

Bordeaux can be used on most native plants except on delicate or new foliage or where the blossom may be spoiled. In hot weather, spray in the cool of night. Repeated applications will be needed in wet weather. Use chamomile or casuarina spray at any time. Most mildew problems are caused by growing the plants in the wrong conditions, usually in too much shade. Repeated light pruning may help, as new growth is more disease and frost resistant. Frost damage can be a precursor of disease. Seaweed sprays every fortnight may also help increase disease resistance. See Sooty mould under Trees and shrubs, pp. 116–17.

GALLS ON LEAVES OR STEMS

These are caused by the larvae of the gall wasp, or by a parasite after the larvae. They rarely harm the tree but can be cut off if necessary. Rosellas, black cockatoos and other birds will eat them.

KURRAJONG LEAF ROLLERS

These dull green caterpillars roll and mat leaves together; the moths are yellow with black markings. Use derris or pyrethrum spray while the caterpillars are young (1 g pyrethrum or derris powder to 1 kg soft soap and 20 L water). Try Dipel.

MOLE CRICKETS

These are dull brown insects with black eyes, about 6 mm long, with strong front legs. They may uproot young plants and seedlings but usually cause minimal damage. If it is absolutely necessary to control crickets, prepare an emulsion of equal parts soft soap and eucalyptus oil. Inject this into tunnels to bring them to the surface, or spread it thickly on the ground around the plant stems to deter them.

PSYLLIDS

This family includes lerp-building nymphs. They are related to aphids and other sap-suckers and create rounded or flat bumps on leaves. Psyllids have a wide range of predators including many birds. There is probably no need to take action against psyllids as they should not reduce the vigour of the tree.

SAWFLIES

Sawfly damage is indicated by skeletonised leaves. Sawflies are wasps, not flies.

Various species of sawfly damage eucalypts, the most common being the steel-blue sawfly, *Perga affinus*, also known as a spitfire. When disturbed, spitfires raise their heads and abdomens and eject a thick yellowish fluid from their mouths. This stings human skin. It probably evolved as a defense against parasitic insects, but makes the nickname most appropriate.

Steel-blue sawfly larvae are black and cluster together around branches. They are about 7 mm long and are mostly laid in summer and autumn.

The larvae of the callitris (callistemon) sawfly, *Zenarge turneri*, are green and 1–2 mm long. Callistemon sawflies feed voraciously, but only on callistemons. They have a sword-like protuberance on their abdomen.

Leaf blister sawflies attack several species of eucalypts. They feed between the upper and lower surface of the leaves so the leaf appears blistered. They mostly affect young trees. Infestations usually only last a season or two then sawflies may disappear for some years.

Control. The first defense against sawflies is to wait for predators. The chief of these are birds, especially cuckoo shrikes and yellow robins. A wide range of wasp species also attack sawflies. Ants are less effective but persistent predators.

If sawflies are badly defoliating the trees, try to shake them down. Use a rake to shake the higher branches. Because of their clustering habit, sawflies are easily dislodged.

You may prefer to prune lower branches that are affected. Wear boots when stamping on sawflies, or let chooks eat them.

Even though sawflies are not true caterpillars (larvae of moths or butterflies), Dipel can be effective against them. Dipel attacks caterpillar intestines and so is harmless to predators. Dipel must be eaten to be effective, so spray the leaf thoroughly, not the sawflies. Derris, pyrethrum or pikelet spray will also kill sawfly larvae, and chilli and tansy sprays will repel them.

SLATERS

These are greyish, flat and many-legged. They shelter during the day and feed on young plant shoots at night.

Try a bait of 1 part pyrethrum to 2 parts flour (either dry or wetted with water). Place bait near wood heaps or rubbish piles where slaters shelter during the day. The best prevention, however, is simply to clean up old wood heaps and piles of rubbish or slow wood chip mulches.

STAGHORN FROND BEETLE

These are small round beetles; their larvae, orange and about a fingertip in size, tunnel into staghorn fronds. Simply cut off the infected fronds or squash the larvae inside and the breeding cycle will be broken.

TERMITES OR WHITE ANTS

These can eat the centre out of trees. Avoid scarring trees near the base as this can provide an entry point. Cut out infected wood and seal with grafting wax, then burn the infected material. Cut down and burn badly infected trees to save others. Try to dig the nests out whole or cover the area with boiling water then spray with pyrethrum.

PROBLEMS

BANKSIA

BANKSIA MOTHS, GREVILLEA LOOPERS, DOUBLE-HEADED HAWK MOTHS, LONGICORN LOOPERS
Symptoms: Chewed leaves.
Solution: Use pyrethrum or Dipel.

BORONIA

Avoid root rots by using a lime-and-phosphorous-free compost mulch, made with lucerne and wattle bark. Well-drained soils are essential. Boronias may die if the soil is too hot or dry; keep trees well mulched.

BOTTLEBRUSH (CALLISTEMON)

CALLISTEMON SAWFLIES
Symptoms: Skeletonised leaves.
Solution: See Sawflies, p. 127.

FAILURE TO FLOWER
This may be caused by lack of direct sunlight.

LEAF SPOT
Solution: Avoid shady areas; spray with chamomile tea after rain or watering. The bush may be in the wrong place.

OTHER PESTS
Galls swell stems; thrips cause leaf curl; moth borers are a problem. See Borers, pp. 125–26.

BRUSH BOX

PSYLLIDS
Symptoms: Masses of powdery white wax; distorted new growth.

Solution: These usually don't cause much harm. Try using a soapy water spray; see Psyllids, pp. 126–27.

FUNGAL LEAF SPOT
Symptoms: Yellow spots on leaves.
Solution: Spray with Bordeaux in severe cases; keep the tree growing strongly.

CABBAGE TREE

CABBAGE TREE MOTHS
Symptoms: The larvae of the cabbage tree moth damage young leaves and the centre of the plant.
Solution: Cut off dead leaves under which the moths rest; try a tansy antifeedant spray; or white pepper spray; spray with Dipel to control the caterpillars, or use derris or pyrethrum spray.

CHRISTMAS BUSH

PHYTOPHTHORA ROOT ROT
Symptoms: Dieback of top branches or whole bush.
Solution: See Root rots, pp. 56–57.

EUCALYPTUS

These are susceptible to sawflies, the larvae of various moths, Christmas beetles, wasp galls and borer. See pp. 125–27. The scribbly gum moth makes its characteristic, harmless designs on eucalypts.

Mistletoe is a common parasite on eucalypts. There are also mistletoes that parasitise other mistletoes. Cut them off if they seem to be affecting the tree.

EUCALYPTUS AND OTHER WEEVILS
Symptoms: Small weevils that chew leaves.

Solution: These should be kept under control by wasps and other predators that parasitise the eggs. Avoid harmful sprays that may eliminate them. In bad cases try a tansy antifeedant spray.

WHITE-STEMMED GUM MOTHS
Symptoms: These large hairy moths have wavy grey-brown markings on their wings. Larvae are about 11 mm long with spiky tufts of hair. They rest behind the bark during the day and feed on leaves at night.
Solution: These should cause little damage if the tree is growing strongly. Wrap sacking round the tree for them to shelter in during the day. Remove and squash; try a tansy antifeedant spray.

GEEBUNG

LEAF SPOT
Solution: Avoid shady positions. Try chamomile, horsetail or garlic spray, or half-strength Bordeaux in temperatures below 24°C; don't spray new growth, flowers or fruit.

GERALDTON WAX

PHYTOPHTHORA ROOT ROT
Symptoms: Dieback, wilted or yellowed leaves.
Solution: Plant in well drained, preferably sandy soil, not in heavy soils. Make sure the roots are not disturbed by digging and the shrub is rarely shaded. Do not mulch, keep other plants away from the base and keep the soil dryish.

GREVILLEA

These are subject to scale, caterpillars and borers. See pp. 115–16, p. 126 and p. 127.
LEAF SPOT
Solution: This is common in some grevilleas

in humid weather. Improve air circulation if possible (often difficult in jungly native gardens). Spray with Bordeaux in temperatures below 24°C; wipe foliage with a wettex dipped in chamomile or chive tea; spray with horsetail tea.

HAKEA

FUNGAL LEAF SPOT
Symptoms: Black spots on leaves.
Solution: See Grevillea, p. 129.

KURRAJONG AND FLAME TREE

KURRAJONG LEAF MOTH
Symptoms: Chewed leaves.
Solution: Try Dipel or garlic spray; dust leaves with white pepper; try a tansy antifeedant spray.

KURRAJONG WEEVIL
Symptoms: Larvae tunnel into woods so look for dying branches, sawdust deposits.
Solution: See Borers, pp. 125–26.

LILLY-PILLY

These are often attacked by scale, which creates associated sooty mould on the leaves. See Scale, pp. 115–16.

MACADAMIA

TWIG GIRDLER
Symptoms: Leaves webbed together.
Solution: Try pyrethrum or Dipel.

MELALEUCA

PAPERBARK SAWFLIES
Symptoms: Chewed leaves, pupae in bark.
Solution: See Sawflies, p. 127.

FUNGAL DIEBACK
Symptoms: New shoots die back.
Solution: This is prevalent in cool, shady areas. Cut off affected shoots; spray with casuarina tea, or Bordeaux in temperatures below 24°C.

MINT BUSH (PROSTANTHERA)

SPINDLY BUSHES
Solution: Prune the tips every year while young, thereafter prune after flowering.

PHYTOPHTHORA ROOT ROT
Symptoms: Dieback.
Solution: Plant in well-drained, preferably gravelly, soil. Mulch with compost but keep compost away from the stem. Never saturate mint bushes with water. If possible, plant bushes grafted onto the coast rosemary, *Westringia fruticosa*, which is resistant to root rot. See Root rots, pp. 56–57.

NORFOLK ISLAND PINE

DIEBACK
These trees are thought to die back on some beachfronts because sewerage pollutants containing detergents are being blown back onto land. Start lobbying for sane sewerage treatment.

PITTOSPORUM

APHIDS AND SCALE
These regularly attack pittosporum. See Aphids, p. 61 and Scale, pp. 115–16.

PITTOSPORUM LEAF MINER
Symptoms: Small, pale, slightly dimpled specks on leaves.

Solution: This insect only disfigures the leaves. Damage is usually barely noticeable and rarely affects the vigour of the tree.

POWDERY MILDEW
Symptoms: Powdery deposits on leaves.
Solution: Try milk spray or combined garlic and chamomile sprays. If these have no effect, try a half-strength Bordeaux in temperatures below 24°C.

THRIPS
See Thrips, pp. 59–60.

TEA TREE (LEPTOSPERMUM)

TEA TREE WEB MOTHS
Symptoms: The larvae of these moths feed on foliage together, sheltering during the day in a mass of webs.
Solution: Prune and burn branches with webs; spray with pyrethrum in soapy water or garlic in soapy water.

SOLDIER BEETLES
These are attracted to the flowers but rarely damage the plant.

SOOTY MOULD
Symptoms: Black deposits on leaves.
Solution: The sweet excretions of scale often cause sooty mould. See Scale, pp. 115–16, and Sooty mould, pp. 116–17.

WARATAH (TELOPEA)

FAILURE TO FLOWER
Waratahs flower on terminal shoots; regular pruning encourages more shoots and flowers.

WATTLE (ACACIA)

Wattles are often short-lived; dieback may simply be the result of old age.

ACACIA SPOTTING BUGS

Symptoms: Streaky brown spots caused by sap-sucking and injection of saliva; leaves may die in a severe attack. The bugs are yellow-brown, about 10 mm long.

Solution: Spray pyrethrum or derris mixed with soapy water.

STEM GALLS

Solution: Cut from the tree and burn.

WASP GALLS

Symptoms: Lumps on leaves.

Solution: Most gall-forming wasps are tiny. Their larvae feed on leaves and pupate inside the gall. Pesticides (organic or not) rarely penetrate to harm them. If really necessary, prune and burn affected foliage. Encourage ants that may predate them.

WATTLE LEAF MINERS

Symptoms: The adults are small moths; the larvae cause the damage, tunnelling into the leaves and making fine thin lines or pink blisters (which eventually die and flake off). The larvae pupate in the blisters.

Solution: Cut off and burn affected leaves.

Spray with pyrethrum in soapy water. (This may have limited effect as the larvae are protected in the leaves.)

WATTLE MEALY BUGS

Symptoms: These oval insects are about 4 mm long, purply-black with white wax stripes. They mostly feed on soft new growth.

Solution: Wattle mealy bugs probably won't cause great harm. Prune affected shoots if necessary.

WATTLE TICK SCALE

Symptoms: These large scale are about 5 mm across, darkening from blue–grey to dark brown. They can be dull or shiny, and are usually grouped together.

Solution: See Scale, pp. 115–16.

WAXFLOWER

WHITE WAX SCALE

Solution: If necessary, try a light oil spray in temperatures below 24°C or spray soapy water in temperatures below 20°C. See Scale, pp. 115–16.

LAWNS

Grass is one of the hardiest plants on earth; many grasses actually suppress the growth of other plants around them. Yet lawns demand more work than any other part of the garden; mowing, watering, feeding and keeping them green and weed free. Most lawn problems occur because we mistreat our lawns.

FIVE CRIMES AGAINST YOUR LAWN

1. USING THE LAWNMOWER AS ROTARY HOE

Many people use their lawnmower as a lethal weapon, like a rotary hoe, not as tool for lawn care. Never mow too deeply; deep mowing controls the shallow-rooted grass but the deep-rooted weeds survive. Deep mowing can slice off the grass roots altogether on small rises, leaving bare spots that weeds will colonise. Grass, like any plant, needs its greenery to feed itself. The shorter it is, the more it has to strain its food and moisture reserves to grow back again.

Treat lawn gently; mow off the grass tips only. If necessary, mow again a few days later. In the long term this is less work than resowing lawn or using herbicide or a mattock

to get rid of weeds. Mowing short grass is easier and quicker than ploughing through long grass. It is the evenness, not the shortness, of the grass that makes it look tidy. Trimmed regularly, a relatively long lawn will look neat. Weeds, which grow faster than grass, make lawns untidy. Light trimming will keep weeds in check by stimulating grass spread and stopping the weeds setting seed.

The timing of lawnmowing is also important. Don't mow your lawn too often in the heat of summer (or it will need more water). Grass roots need a healthy growth on top to insulate them against the heat. Do mow often in spring and autumn. Unfortunately spring and autumn are the seasons when most gardeners put away the lawnmowers but they are actually the most crucial times to mow. Many annual weeds will be setting seed. If they are not mowed they'll spread their seed. A late autumn mow and an early spring trim will stimulate your grass to keep on spreading and will set back weeds as well.

During winter, if your lawn looks uneven, mow it. Often the weeds will grow while the grass has stopped, so an occasional run over with the lawnmower will keep the weeds from setting seed and spreading.

Don't mow when the temperature is above 35°C. Wait until the cool of the evening to mow, then water immediately afterwards. Don't mow wet grass; it will tear.

2. STRIP-MINING THE LAWN

Every time you take away a barrow of clippings you're strip-mining nutrients and moisture and organic matter from the lawn. All of these need to be replaced or the lawn will starve or become patchy.

If you mow your lawn regularly and don't take off too much at once (a neat trim rather than a solid shearing) the lawnmower won't leave great ugly clumps of mown grass around, and the faint trails will disappear within a couple of days. Choose a 'mulching' style of lawnmower without a catcher. If the lawnmower is designed to spit grass into a catcher, let the clippings dry out for a day then scatter them evenly over the grass.

Different grasses need to be mown to different lengths. Couch and bent grass do best at about 15 mm. Kikuyu needs to be somewhat higher and should be mown once a week or more, or it will become stalky, rather than leafy. Rye grass and Kentucky blue grass and many other warm-climate grasses do best at about 40 mm or more.

3. THE GRAB AND GROW TECHNIQUE

Don't make your lawn from the first bag of lawn seed found on the supermarket garden shelves. Australia has many climates and a grass that grows best in one area doesn't necessarily grow well in another location. Check your neighbourhood for lawns which do well in winter and summer without being fussed over every second day. Find out what sort of grasses or grass and clover mix they contain. Most lawns do best with a mixture of grasses, or grasses and clovers. Grass is green in summer and clover is green in cooler weather.

4. STARVING THE LAWN

I don't approve of diets for me or my lawn. Lawns are healthiest when well fed. Your lawn should require almost no extra feeding once it is well established, if the clippings are left; the nutrients and organic matter will just recycle.

Feeding the lawn:

• Sprinkle lightly with dryish compost; if sieved, it will disappear after the first good watering. In warm weather, compost will disappear by itself within a week.

• Top dress with good soil (good for compacted lawns, or to even up small hollows).

• Scatter on dry, sieved or pelletised hen manure, or blood and bone. The smell vanishes soon after watering, if the application is not too heavy. Too much may burn the lawn or kill the earthworms and other soil life. Scatter it very gently (like putting icing sugar on a cake) and repeat in a month if the lawn needs more feeding. A scatter of hen manure every five years or so is enough to keep lawn green and healthy if the clippings are left.

• If lawn clippings are used elsewhere, feed the lawn twice a year: a gentle scatter in spring and midsummer. Many proprietary lawn feeds are low in phosphorous. In a phosphorous-deficient lawn the clover will not grow well, and the grass will have a purply tinge (especially couch grass, which needs quite large amounts of phosphorous).

• Lawn fed with either compost or hen manure should not require added phosphorous. If necessary, scatter rock phosphate every five years or so.

5. OVERWATERING THE LAWN

Frequent watering will not necessarily result in a green lawn. Overwatered lawn may be affected by cold or require extra feeding; excess watering wastes a scarce resource and encourages fungus diseases. It will also encourage shallow roots which have no resistance in a heat wave.

Train your lawn to develop deeper roots. Let it dry out between waterings and ensure that water soaks deeply, so that as the surface moisture dries out, the roots will penetrate deeper and deeper. Use a fine spray to water. Puddles on the lawn will mostly evaporate and the soil below will compact, so that even less water penetrates. Soils rich in organic matter hold water better.

PROBLEMS

MOSS AND ALGAE

Do not water too often; try to improve drainage. Water the area with 1 teaspoon copper sulphate dissolved in 45 L water.

PATCHY LAWN

This may be because the wrong grass has been planted. If the lawn is usually patchy in winter or summer, consider resowing.

If traffic is creating patchy lawn, consider a path, or stepping stones, or a tougher variety of grass. (Grass often wears out between house and sheds or washing line, etc.) Another alternative is to lay down flat rocks or rounds of wood at close intervals. These will not disturb the lawn's smooth appearance as a formal path might. Avoid straight paths; most people naturally walk in a slightly curved line, and straight paths break up the appearance of a garden. Do not curve the path too much or people will cut across it.

Patches are also caused by petrol spilled on the lawn or dog or cat urine. Use dog or cat repellent and water well.

Various fungi may also cause patchy lawns. See Diseases, pp. 135–36.

TREES

Lawns do not grow well under trees; the branches shade the grass and the roots compete with it. Many grasses will inhibit the growth of trees' small roots; trunk injury from mowing around trees is a common beginning of disease, which enters through the resulting wound.

Avoid grass under trees. Fill the space instead with violets, strawberries, or a formal garden bed with shade-loving plants. To create a park-like appearance, with grass right up to the tree trunks, prune the lower branches so that the grass gets more light, and regularly top dress under the tree with new soil.

PESTS

CORBIE MOTHS

Symptoms: These moth larvae can create bare areas that get colonised by weeds. Their tunnels are lined with webs. Damage is worst in late autumn or early spring, when the grass is not growing.

Solution: Encourage large birds such as magpies. Use 1 part pyrethrum spray to 2 parts water with just enough detergent so that the water lathers a little. Don't use detergent too often, as it can kill grass roots. Try a heavy spray of Dipel at night. Use a port wine trap (see Codling moth control, pp. 52–53) will also trap corbie moths. As a last resort, try one of the synthetic pyrethrins.

COUCHTIP MAGGOTS

Symptoms: These eat out the growing tips, so the grass never really gets growing properly. The pest may be unnoticeable, but watch for small clouds of flies when walking on the grass.

Solution: Let the grass grow quite long, then mow off a few millimetres every few days. Carefully spray pyrethrum and eucalyptus on the tips of the grass.

COUCHGRASS MITES

Symptoms: The topmost grass leaves look bunchy or deformed.

Solution: Mites like dry places; water lawn well. If it is growing under walls where rainfall may not penetrate, try growing another lawn type there.

GRASS-WEBBING MITES

Symptoms: Large, bleached circles in the grass, often covered in webs.

Solution: Use wettable sulphur, 2 g per 1 L water. Anise and coriander sprays may also be effective; cover the spice with boiling water, leave until cool and spray at night.

LAWN ARMY WORMS

Symptoms: These are moth caterpillars which eat leaves and stems. They are brown to greenish-brown, with stripey bodies, and love paspalum, couch and kikuyu.

Solution: Spray with Dipel or a pyrethrum spray. Add compost to encourage mycelium webs, earthworms and a range of soil fungi that can help control them.

WHITE CURL GRUBS (COCKCHAFERS)

Symptoms: Bare patches as grass is sheared off at ground level. These beetle larvae can vary in size, are white, and curl up when exposed. They eat grass roots (and sometimes leaves) and strawberry roots.

Solution: Encourage large birds such as magpies and kookaburras. Top dress with compost to encourage predacious insects and microorganisms. Companion planting with mustard may help, but is usually impractical. As a last resort, try one of the synthetic pyrethrins.

DISEASES

DAMPING OFF

Symptoms: Grass pales or dies in circles, new plants look distorted. Damping off is worst in moist, wet or humid weathe.

Solution: Avoid high-nitrogen fertilisers, and add a little rock phosphate. Water well with strong chamomile tea. Fertilise with blood and bone in spring.

FUSARIUM DRY PATCH

Symptoms: Dry patch fungi break down the dead grass and make the soil water-repellent. The grass may be water stressed or look patchy.

Solution: Dry patch is worst in sandy soils. Sprinkle the lawn with compost and increase the organic matter in the soil. In the short term, fork the lawn well to let water penetrate. Use an agricultural wetter, or a detergent; be careful with domestic detergents as they can kill grass roots.

FUSARIUM PATCH

Symptoms: This is a winter, wet-weather disease. The grass turns yellow and looks slimy.

Solution: Avoid high-nitrogen fertilisers. Sprinkle a little potash over the lawn every autumn. Do not mow affected grass. A regular seaweed or strong garlic spray will help grass resistance. Dust with sieved compost in autumn.

KIKUYU YELLOWS

Symptoms: The grass roots rot and the lawn turns yellow in circular spreading patches. This is worst in wet, hot weather.

Solution: Improve drainage, add more organic matter to the soil with compost or with even, finely sprinkled, well-chopped mulch.

LEAF SPOT

Symptoms: Grass turns dark grey and the leaves look blotchy.

Solution: Give one generous sprinkle of hen manure and weekly sprays of seaweed spray for a month.

OPHIOBOLUS PATCH

Symptoms: This affects bent grass, forming great, wide, patchy circles.

Solution: Avoid liming; add compost or a scatter of shredded pine needles in alkaline areas. Increase the organic level of the soil with compost or a finely chopped mulch spread over the lawn. Give a scatter of hen manure, and stop leaving lawn clippings. Improve drainage.

RED THREAD

Symptoms: Grass mottles; the red threads of the fungus may be visible in the dead patches.
Solution: Feed grass with a scatter of hen manure, watered in well.

RUST

Symptoms: Grass can become brown to orange–red; the orange–red spores are just visible on the leaves.
Solution: Keep lawn growing well with regular feeding and mowing. Soaking with 1 aspirin dissolved in 5 glasses of water may help. Sprinkle on compost.

LAWN WEEDS

Lawns usually get weeds because they are not growing well. Weeds may result from an extended drought, visits by neighbourhood dogs or skateboarders, or other lawn hazards which are difficult to avoid.

The best way to control lawn weeds is to mow your lawn regularly. This stops any annual weeds from seeding. Grasses do well if mown regularly as weeds prefer to grow long and lanky. After all, most grasses were regularly munched by grazing animals before suburban lawn weeds existed, but weeds became weeds because animals do not like to eat them.

Other lawn weeds can be cut out with a sharp trowel (attach it to a long stick to avoid having to stoop). Most weeds can be killed with boiling water or with the urine or sulphate of ammonia treatment for deep-rooted weeds described under Dandelion, p. 26. For shallow-rooted weeds use the methods described under Bindii, p. 135.

SOME PERSISTENT WEEDS

BINDII

Before they become prickly, these show up bright green against the darker green grass in late winter and early spring. Scatter on sulphate of ammonia or two-day-old undiluted urine. Do not water for two days. Alternately, just pour boiling water on bindiis.

DANDELIONS

To remove, stick a stake deep into the plant and pour boiling water down the resultant hole.

OXALIS

This often grows where grass cover is insufficient to keep it in check, under trees for example. Oxalis can be choked out by planting daisies or some other ground cover next to them. Even violets can be effective. Dig out oxalis in late winter when its food reserves are low.

PASPALUM

One blow with a mattock will remove this; roots left in the soil will not regenerate.

PLANTAIN

A quick swipe of the mattock will kill plantain and is easier than spraying herbicide.

INDEX